LOCUS

LOCUS

LOCUS

LOCUS

Taiwan Prospect

Sayling Wen

Illustrated by Chih-Chung Tsai

Tomorrow Studio's Declaration

Human beings are what make the changes and advances of history possible. Creation, destruction, success and failure all come from humans and human actions. It is in human nature to challenge limits and strive for a better future.

It is our belief that all human beings share the dream and hope of freeing themselves from the narrowness of individualism, blood relationships, and regionalism so that they can travel freely in space and time to create a better future. This belief is why a great number of elite people have joined hands to form a professional writers group - Tomorrow Studio. All of us at Tomorrow Studio expect to contribute good books to foster that dream and to benefit the future of human beings.

There are two definitions for "ming-ri" (literally bright day.) One is simply "tomorrow." Future dreams and goals sound very remote; yet tomorrow seems more real and more tangible. If we want to create a better tomorrow, we should start today. The other definition of "ming-ri" is "to know what is intended for oneself and to be a new person every day."

To know what is intended for oneself is to know the past and the future; to know ethics, civilization, and the rules of the world; to have ideals and goals. It is to utilize human beings' property - our accumulated knowledge and collected wisdom - and to abide by long established moral standards.

To be a new person every day is to rid oneself of old errors and drawbacks, to gain new knowledge, to learn new skills, to better oneself, and to strive for a brighter future day after day.

Three centuries ago, Newton said, "If I have seen further, it is by standing on the shoulders of giants." Accumulated knowledge and collected wisdom are the common property of human beings and, therefore, what Newton meant by "giant's shoulders." To know what is intended for oneself is to better utilize the giants' shoulders and to abide by moral legacy. To become a new person every day is to constantly strive for a better tomorrow. The aforementioned are the ideals of Tomorrow Studio and the guidelines for our publications. We welcome people who share our ideals and our dreams to come join us to help create a brighter tomorrow.

Acknowledgments

How many times can a person witness a new millennium in his lifetime?

How many times can a person expect to encounter a serious financial storm in his lifetime?

And, how many times can a person expect to experience an economic miracle in his lifetime?

At present, many of us living in Taiwan still feel the effects of the East Asia financial storm of the late 1990s. However, as we cross over to the years 2000 and 2001, we begin to look forward to Taiwan's second economic miracle.

Foreword
Sharing Knowledge and Information
By Lien Chan

(Vice President, Republic of China)

Facing this pivotal moment of crossing over into the 21st century, spurred ahead by political democratization, social pluralization and economic liberalization, the people and government on Taiwan are working hand in hand to create brighter development prospects. We firmly believe that, by adding creativity and vitality to our sincere practical efforts, we can unleash ceaseless energy to meet every challenge and enter the group of developed nations.

Looking back on years past, we have all made efforts to forge an economic achievement that is the envy of the world. In weighing the future and planning the right development policy, we must rely on the thoughts and experiences of people in all walks of life in addition to working together. In this process, the sharing of knowledge and information is crucial. My schoolmate, Mr. Sayling Wen, Vice Chairman of Inventec Group, is a graduate of both the affiliated school of National Taiwan Normal University and National Taiwan University. He has made full use of his keen observations, deep analyses, advanced views, fluid writing style, as well as abundant expertise and rich practical experience, to write this book, *Taiwan Prospect*. His book provides us with essential contents, unique revelations and many observations to stimulate our thoughts and guide our efforts into the future. This book warrants deep reflection.

In early and mid-March of 1998, I visited the Inventec Group factories in Penang, Malaysia, and Lin-kou, Taiwan. I came away from both visits with a deep impression of this company's approach to management, and so I felt delighted to write a preface for this book the moment I saw it. My ancestor, Lien Ya-tang wrote in the "Preface" to General History of Taiwan: Great indeed were our ancestors. They crossed the great sea and entered this wilderness. They plowed and cultivated the soil for the benefit of their sons and grandsons for the next ten thousand years. Their efforts were a grand endeavor. Reflecting back on their virtue, their concern for the future was as if they were entering a deep valley full of caution.

Our ancestors' endeavor provided today's generation with a foundation to build upon in striving to advance forward and create Taiwan's second economic miracle. This is indeed our expectation as we cross over to the new century. Ah, maternal sea, ah, beautiful island, stable and prosperous, let's work to fulfill our dream.

Foreword
A Trigger to Stimulate a New Beginning
By John C. I. Ni

(Director General Small and Medium Enterprise Administration
Ministry of Economic Affairs / Member of the National Assembly,
R. O. C.)

Born in Taiwan in the 1950s, Mr. Sayling Wen grew up in a lovely home, and breezed through elementary school, middle school, high school, and college with little effort. He entered the field of electronic engineering just at the time when Taiwan was creating its first economic miracle. Together with seven partners, he established a business and has been working diligently for some 23 years. Step by step the company has developed into the prominent transnational "group" it is today, with a workforce of some 8,400 employees. Mr. Wen uses his sharp mind to make keen observations, and formulate unique concepts. His writings and explanations offer us a vast horizon for reflection. His words are a trigger to stimulate our new beginning.

Taiwan Prospect contains no long-winded, self-centered ramblings. The author portrays the bitter struggle behind our past successes and the hidden dangers behind the optimistic prospects. He presents all sorts of phenomena to stimulate deep thought, reminding us of the great cost we have to pay once we carelessly make a false step and start to head off in the wrong direction.

The figures to be proud of and the achievements to be envious of all were created over the past decades through the joint efforts of government and its people. But, facing the new Network Age of instant calculation, how can we make plans and implement them in this glorious new era? How can we bring our excellent economic position into play? How can we cultivate and develop our accumulated experience and wisdom? Read this book carefully and think deeply about the ideas and suggestions put forward.

As part of my work, which provides counseling services for small and medium enterprises, I have had the good fortune of inviting an outstanding schoolmate of mine to speak at two meetings. Mr. Sayling Wen, a graduate of the affiliated school of National Taiwan Normal University and National Taiwan University, titled his topic for the meetings: "Again, Creating Taiwan's Second Miracle." The meetings were "Workshop 3 - Guidance and Assistance Program for Small and Medium Enterprises" (March 12, 1997) and "Projection & Strategy Conference for Small & Medium Enterprises" (December 22, 1997). Mr. Wen's speeches were clear, to the point and yet far-reaching. The participants in these meetings were moved and persuaded by his ideas. Now he has compiled these lectures into a book. I am delighted that more people will have the opportunity to read his pearls of wisdom. Therefore, I have written a few words to express my sincere appreciation and high regard for him.

Contents

Preface

Back in 1972, I served as a factory manager in Er-chung-pu, Taipei County. Every day for lunch I had to squeeze into a cafeteria smaller than a classroom stuffed with 160 employees. When I sat down, my back would nearly lean up against the back of the employee seated behind me.

Ordinarily, before we started to eat, I would rise, say a few words, and reemphasize the goal of the month. Next, the foreman on duty that day would report to everybody on our progress towards meeting our monthly production target. After that, all the employees would shout their determination to meet the production target. Finally, the factory Vice Manager would shout, "Commence eating!" and everybody would dig into their own NT$1.5 lunch box of tiny fish, dried bean curd and vegetables with relish. After eating and taking a brief siesta, everybody would return to the production line to resume his difficult, dangerous work with determination. I remember that once, for the sake of completing a very large rush order, for three days and nights I didn't sleep in a bed! Many colleagues also worked overtime late into the night. Several who had trouble coping and thus became overly exhausted were given a traditional elixir of brown sugar and ginger powder in hot water so that they could carry on.

Those were unforgettable times! All across Taiwan small and medium enterprises were springing up in this kind of environment. There were few complaints and no protests; everyone was striving for a better life. Without really knowing it, they eventually defeated poverty and forged Taiwan's first economic miracle.

Today, in the 1990s, the youth living in Taiwan should feel fortunate to have fashionable clothes, fine food and a general lack of privation. When, by chance, they happen to see a film describing Taiwan's difficult path to economic development, they feel it is just "ancient history," with no specific relevance to them. However, I often think that if I were a youth of today, I too would feel confused. Why do these adults who had grown up in adversity, stress the "outward exodus of industry and gloomy economic prospects," on the one hand, appear to pursue money blindly and participate actively in political farce and ball game cheating, on the other.

Taiwan's society went through several significant

changes in the recent past, as Ta-you Lo likes to describe in his folk songs. What things should we hold up to our youth as models to emulate? After all, despite the disorder in Taiwan's society and the pessimistic words that are bantered about, we can still see reason for hope: we can see conditions present for the possibility of creating Taiwan's second economic miracle. The purpose of this book is to discuss a new turning point. We firmly hope that this new generation of youth can see that Taiwan is at a new turning point and thus rise to play leading roles as we embark on this challenging new voyage.

In *Taiwan Experience*, I described in detail Taiwan's economic development over the past fifty years. In this book, I first look back at the thirty-year period from the 60s to the 90s-at how Taiwan's government and enterprises had together created what is today called the first economic miracle. I then go on to discuss how we could realize a new turning point in Taiwan's productive enterprises after the 1990s, after our traditional industries have moved overseas, mostly to China, and after our own manufacturers have seemingly vanished into a black hole.

Next, I go on to discuss, how a new wealth-creating

system based on the principle of "using knowledge to create wealth" is beginning to appear, in the midst of rapid changes in Taiwan's social environment, in addition to the occurrence of new phenomena. I also explain what sorts of new industries and future developments we can expect to see. At the end of this book, I outline "Taiwan's second economic miracle," describe the direction of that development trend, and suggest how government and people can work together to realize it.

When some of my old teachers, schoolmates and friends heard that I was writing this book on how to create Taiwan's second economic miracle, they immediately offered to share with me their valuable ideas drawn from their various areas of expertise. It is impossible for me to express my appreciation to each of them by listing names individually. But, I especially want to extend my appreciation to my schoolmate Lien Chan for taking time out from his very busy life as Vice President to visit our factories in Malaysia and Taipei County. He made many impressive observations during his visits. I also would like to thank the Director General of Small and Medium Enterprises Administration, Ministry of Economic Affairs, Mr. John

C. I. Ni. For many years, we have shared ideas about management concepts, as well as the joys of growing up. These two people were the first to see the manuscript of this book. So, I am delighted and deeply thankful they were willing to take time out of their busy schedules to write forwards for me.

The First Movement: Looking Back

People must sometimes look back on the past in order to draw knowledge and courage from past experiences. In this way, they will have extra wisdom when facing future opportunities.

Before 1960, Taiwan was a poor rural society: during the thirty-year period from 1960 to 1990, the government and the people worked shoulder to shoulder through many adversities when hundreds of things were waiting to be done, to create the first economic miracle.

Taiwan's First Economic Miracle (1960-1990)

Taiwan's first economic miracle that occurred between 1960 and 1990 was based on its transformation from an agricultural economy to an industrial one. During these thirty years, its economy grew as follows:

	1960	1970	1980	1990
Monthly Wage	US$2 - 3	US$10	US$100	US$800
GDP Per Capita	US$150	US$400	US$2,300	US$8,000
Export Value	US$200m	US$2b	US$20b	US$80b
Foreign Exchange Reserves	US$76 m	US$1b (1975)	US$5.3b	US$80b

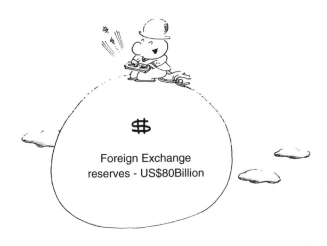

Foreign Exchange
reserves - US$80Billion

The above chart shows how our government and many enterprises worked together to create an economic miracle during those thirty years. Looking back now, it was not at all easy to achieve this miracle.

In 1949 when the Nationalist Government evacuated from the Chinese mainland and came over to Taiwan, the political, economic and social conditions here were not very promising. Yet, by facing those adverse conditions, we managed to learn valuable lessons during those initial ten years. Taiwan's politics and society gradually stabilized and formed a good foundation for subsequent economic development.

The year when Taiwan's small and medium enterprises began to take off was 1960. At that time, the average wage was just US$2-3, or NT$80-120, per month! During that time, the government fixed the exchange rate between the New Taiwan dollar and the US dollar at 40:1. The per capita income was just US$150, export value was US$200 million, and foreign exchange reserves totaled US$76 million. By today's standards, those figures do not look very impressive, but for the small and medium enterprises of the day, that provided a good starting point.

Ten years later, in 1970, monthly income rose to

NT$400, or US$10. Per capita income reached US$400 per year and export value reached US$2 billion.

In 1975, we created our first US$1 billion of foreign exchange reserves. At that time, that was an extraordinary record.

We can discern that during the period from 1960 to 1970 small and medium businesses grew vigorously. The following decade was even more important.

By 1980, monthly average wage had risen to US$100 while per capita income had leaped to US$2,300. Export value grew 10 times, reaching US$20 billion, and foreign exchange reserves were US$5.3 billion. But, this foreign exchange reserves figure did not tell the whole story because many manufacturers deposited their foreign exchange holdings overseas.

From 1989 to the middle of the 1990s, a big change took place. After 1986, the New Taiwan dollar appreciated from 40:1 to 26/27:1 against the US dollar. This caused great consternation among many local enterprises. This rapid valuation of the NT dollar caused an equally rapid reduction in the profits of manufacturers that earned foreign currency.

The small and medium enterprises blazed
a way in the midst of hardship and created
Taiwan's first economic miracle.

Despite this situation, we continued to enjoy steady economic growth. In 1990, our average wage reached US$800 per month, our per capita income rose to US$8,000, and our export value was US$80 billion. Because of the appreciation of the New Taiwan dollar and continued political stability, we greatly surpassed our foreign exchange reserves target amount. Public confidence in the country increased greatly and many manufacturers returned their foreign exchange holdings back to Taiwan, and that was a lot of money. This continuous influx of foreign exchange holdings into the country soon made us the world's second or third holder of foreign exchange.

As a consequence, however, because so much foreign currency came back to Taiwan, Taiwan's entire society became awash in money. And, because everyone had money, people began to speculate in real estate, lotteries, and stocks as well as in all sorts of high stakes money games. Presently, this situation has changed little.

By 1997, our monthly wage had already reached US$12,000-calculated, of course, on the basis of the 27:1 exchange rate. Even if we were to calculate this figure according to the 32:1 exchange rate of 1998, our average monthly wage would still exceed US$1,000. In addition, our average per capita income already exceeded US$15,000. Our export value surpassed US$100 billion and foreign exchange reserves surpassed US$80 billion.

From the late 1980s to the early 1990s, our real foreign exchange reserves far surpassed our target figure of US$80 billion, because during that period our enterprises had begun to make a lot of overseas investments.

Before 1990, Taiwan basically had been a country that received investments. At that time, John C. I. Ni served in the Industrial Development & Investment Center, responsible for strongly promoting Taiwan as one of the best places to invest in. But, from the late

1980s to the early 1990s, Taiwan transformed into an investment and technology exporting country, exporting large-scale investments and technology to Southeast Asia and China, and thus forging a new economic arrangement.

In the meanwhile, Taiwan's economy did not experience any slowdown, and we are still continuing to enjoy healthy growth.

We are really moved by this sort of growth record: in a period of thirty years, our average monthly wage has risen from US$10 to $1,000 — an increase of 100 times in total!

Naturally, our high level growth in per capita income brought along changes in the social environment. Manpower and material resources became much more costly than before and the capital overhead for manufacturing became extremely high because of this. Under these new circumstances, we naturally couldn't continue to manage our enterprises in the traditional ways.

In any country that experiences big changes in labor cost and social values, no enterprise-whether small, medium or large-can continue to use old management methods. For this reason, for the sake of continued growth and development, or even just for the sake of surviving in the new economic environment, every enterprise has to change and adapt its pattern of operations. Over the past ten years, Taiwan's manufacturers have struck out in the direction of their new pattern of operations. This also tells us that Taiwan's enterprises and economy have already set off on a new direction of achieving growth.

First, I want to analyze the reasons for the success of the first economic miracle. Naturally, there were many reasons for this success, so I will start by discussing government assistance.

Government Assistance

The main conductor of Taiwan's first economic miracle was the government. At that time, the government carried out extensive improvements in Taiwan's economic infrastructure under extremely difficult circumstances. Several of the government's main measures had a great effect on Taiwan's economic development.

They included:

(Foreign Trade Reform)

In 1960, the government enacted foreign trade reform. At that time, the exchange rate of the New Taiwan dollar was fixed at 40:1 against the US dollar, which benefited exports. Afterwards, measures such as tax on bonded goods, tax rebates, incentive prizes, were taken. Such measures together created a favorable environment for conducting foreign sales.

(Attracting Foreign Investment)

Next, the government dispatched many outstanding

people overseas to attract foreign investment in Taiwan. Under this program, a number of reputable foreign companies, such as GE and RCA, invested in Taiwan.

(Establishing Export-Processing Zones: 1966)

The systematic change in Taiwan brought about by this influx of foreign investment was something like the change from the old system of purely independent street hawkers to a system of centrally managed street venders.

In order to attract foreign investment in Taiwan, since 1966 we have established three export-processing zones. At the time, we humorously referred to these export-processing zones as big labor camps. In fact, however, this method of attracting foreign investment was of larger scale and has become an important model for developing countries. The idea of export-processing zones was our government's precious contribution to development theory and practice.

(Establishing the China External Trade Development

Council)

Next, the government established the China External Trade Development Council. This Institute provided the place and means to settle trade disputes. This permanent organization was also responsible for coordinating export sales planning, so that individual manufacturers no longer needed to enter foreign markets on their own, to fend for themselves and feel blindly. This service greatly eased the overall development of foreign trade operations.

(Establishing the Industrial Technology Research Institute - 1973)

In 1973, the government established the Industrial Technology Research Institute. Starting out with the universities in Hsin-chu as its nucleus, this Institute was intended to nurture technologists so that Taiwan would have a sufficient pool of qualified manpower. The contribution of this Institute to Taiwan's economic development has been incalculable, especially since the Electronic Research & Service Organization (ERSO) was added in 1974, followed by an IC Model

Factory. These institutions brought Taiwan into step with the latest trends and development leads in electronics technology. At the same time, they provided the foundation for the formation of our semi-conductor industry.

(Promoting the Ten Major Constructions: 1974)

Next, in 1974, President Chiang Ching-kuo promoted the Ten Major Constructions Project. This extremely important project was aimed at improving Taiwan's overall infrastructure. The Ten Major Constructions Project provided all of Taiwan's industrial manufacturers with smooth channels of communication and transport for every aspect of their material production. It accelerated the circulation of materials for every trade and occupation and established a framework for Taiwan's subsequent modernization.

(Establishing the Science-based Industrial Park: 1979)

In 1979, the science-based industrial park was established. If we refer to the export processing zones as giant labor camps, then the science-based industrial park was a great think tank. The export-processing zones served to concentrate Taiwan's productivity. In similar fashion the science-based industrial park centralized Taiwan's technical wizardry. Besides helping to upgrade the level of our local technology, the science-based industrial park also strengthened our research and development capability. In addition, the science-based industrial park also attracted many overseas students and scholars back to Taiwan. These talented people brought back state-of-the-art technology and management methods of international caliber needed to bring about rapid advances in our technology industry.

(Establishing the Institute for Information Industry (III) and Strengthening the China Productivity Center)

Next, the government established the Institute for Information Industry (III) and strengthened the China Productivity Center. These permanent national organizations have played important roles in research and development. Their research and development efforts are focused on new advanced technology and management concepts. They have been cooperating closely with manufacturers, by actually participating in production operations, by saving the investment capital of private units, by helping individual enterprises improve their internal management systems, and so forth. These organizations thus have made great contributions in helping domestic manufacturers upgrade their internal operations in a relatively short time.

Efforts of the People

Naturally, besides the vigorous promotions of concerned government agencies, the efforts and hard work of the people also contributed to creating Taiwan's first economic miracle. They cannot be overlooked. During the thirty-year period between 1960 and 1990, private enterprises in Taiwan displayed vitality, versatility and uncommon entrepreneurial spirit. Generally speaking, the efforts of Taiwan's people moved in several directions:

(Exploitation of Basic Ability: Manpower)

During Taiwan's initial steps toward the Industrial

Age starting in 1960, the main power we relied upon was exploitation of our basic ability, that is, manpower. In the past, when we spoke of industrial management, we spoke of the "3Ms": material, market, and money. Afterwards, when we started to factor in manpower, it became the "4Ms." Subsequently, people spoke of the "7Ms", adding in management, machines, and method. Finally, we began to speak of the 8 or 9 Ms! But, in the very beginning, we just had "1M" manpower. It was our diligence and hard-working spirit that helped us to overcome all the hardships. It was with this most basic, most primitive form of power that we transformed Taiwan from an Agricultural Society into an Industrial one.

(Small Scale Enterprises Take-off, Living Rooms Converted into Factories)

Our small-scale enterprises began to take off soon thereafter. At first factories did outsource work and service for foreign investors, and some small trading companies served as distributors for foreign products.

At that time, there was the saying; "The living room is a factory." People indeed used their own living rooms as factories. When they weren't busy on the farm, or after work, they would do finishing work at home on foreign products, such as clothes and plastic products. For a few dollars or cents reward, people would use their own living rooms to earn some profit for their families and, in effect, for the whole society. It can be said that at times, "every man was armed." Everyone had joined the struggle and was paying with effort. We can see that the struggles of our small and medium enterprises provide vivid testimony of the efforts of the people to succeed.

(Wild Chicken Style Sales)

Once when I was giving a speech in Southeast Asia, people in the audience kept asking me one main question: They said they understood how we in Taiwan strove to create industry, develop the economy, and create products. They understood those sorts of efforts. What they couldn't understand was how we managed to sell the things that we made. How could we find purchasers for our products? In my opinion, the answer lay in our unique Taiwanese "wild chicken style sales."

At that time, many sales representatives of trading companies and factories always brought their product samples and catalogs to the airport, even to hotel lobbies, to show foreigners. No matter the reason the foreigners happened to be there, these traders would try to speak with them to ask whether or not they were interested in placing orders for any of their products. Naturally, they met with many rejections, for they frequently misjudged the foreigners. However, by taking the chance to speak with many people, they could find some interested buyers. This situation reminds me of the old days when we could find "wild chicken" tour buses parked around the city train stations, offering transportation everywhere around the island. When you passed by that area, their people would approach and ask you where you wanted to go, and then they would explain their special route. That was what we called "wild chicken style sales." I think that few people nowadays can imagine that people in Taiwan at that time used such methods to initiate our trade and sell our products.

(IPO and OEM)

Gradually, we produced more products and

achieved a certain level of quality. At that point, several foreign manufacturers started to set up IPOs (International Purchasing Offices) in Taiwan, which allowed Taiwan enterprises to have more systematic sales and enjoy larger scale business. Consequently, our factories, equipment and labor all started to reach a certain standard. Once our products began to be accepted by foreign businesses, several foreign manufacturers started to commission us to manufacture their products because of our lower overhead, especially our relatively inexpensive hard-working labor. This is called an OEM (Original Equipment Manufacturing).

(Textiles, Plastics, Appliances, Steel, etc., and the Formation of First Generation Entrepreneurs)

In the early 1980s, Taiwan became the world's leader in the manufacturing of many kinds of products, such as sports shoes, bicycles, and umbrellas. With the previous twenty years of growth and accumulated wealth, many textiles, plastics, appliances, and steel enterprises had reached international-scale production. At this time, as well, our first entrepreneurs began to appear.

(Electronics, Information, Semiconductors, and the Formation of Second Generation Entrepreneurs)

At the start of the 1990s, the manufacturing of hi-tech products in electronics, telecommunications, and semi-conductors became Taiwan's new major development trend. Several hi-tech enterprises gathered talent from Taiwan's first batch of highly trained technologists. They depended on these technologists' strong determination and indomitable spirit in struggling to compete on par with the leading hi-tech enterprises of the world. In the process, they not only created an unprecedented enterprise structure in Taiwan, they also created a new generation of entrepreneurs with an even more global vision.

(Manufacturers' Overseas Exodus: Exporting Investment Capital and Technology)

Regarding Taiwan's development during the past several years, many local industries had no way to upgrade and make their operations here profitable.

Thus, they had to emigrate overseas in order to find less expensive labor and material resources therefore reducing their capital overhead. As a matter of fact, when these manufacturers moved overseas, they were not giving up on Taiwan; they were exporting investment capital and technology overseas in order to create more wealth outside of Taiwan.

(Appreciation of the New Taiwan Dollar, Money Games, and The Loss of GSP)

It is noteworthy that in 1987, three major events rocked Taiwan's society, one after the other: the rapid appreciation of the NT dollar, the sudden popularity of money games, and the loss of the GSP (Generalized System of Preferences).

The "Everybody Happy" lottery, real estate, the stock market, and similar money games became all the rage, and many people got caught up in fantasies of easy wealth. They busied themselves all day asking oracles for lucky numbers and investments and looking everywhere for land or stocks to invest in. They became less willing to work and, what's more, they began to hold a different view of money than they had during the previous thirty-year period of hard work. This happened once people realized that they could earn more money through one lucky speculation than they could during a lifetime of hard work. Consequently, people became less willing to put in an honest day's work. Taiwan society's preoccupation with such money games caused a sudden erosion in its once touted productivity. Many factories couldn't find suitable employees anymore and all sorts of productive operations stalled. These several social factors also were reasons behind the large-scale overseas exodus of local manufacturers.

This mass exodus of Taiwan's manufacturers could be described as entrepreneurs escaping to foreign lands for their own profit, but viewed from another angle this phenomenon shows that Taiwan had already successfully become thoroughly industrialized. At that time, we ceased depending solely on exporting products; we were starting to export investment capital and technology.

The Second Movement: A New Wealth-creating System

Technology is a blessing. It provides us with unexpected opportunities from which to choose. Technology is also a necessary trend. Like it or not, global technology will act like the rear wave that surges and drives the initial wave ahead; it will cover over the entire past. We can ride this new tide of technology to create our own opportunities. On the other hand, if we don't act quickly enough, we will just drown in this new flood of technology.

Creating Wealth from Knowledge

Few people noticed, but something very important in this world happened in 1996: the total share value on the stock market of two American companies, the computer chip producer Intel and the software producer Microsoft surpassed the total value of America's big three auto makers, General Motors, Ford, and Chrysler. America's big three automakers are in fact the three biggest carmakers in the world. They possess seemingly countless factories and service centers around the world. The amount of steel and other material resources they use in producing cars defies the imagination. The products and capital of Intel and Microsoft are entirely different than those of the traditional auto industry, which requires vast amounts of investment capital, material resources and land.

Intel's product is computer chips. Computer chips are produced by refining inexpensive rock. In fact, the material itself has no value, but the tiny things made by oxidizing silicone out of it-each one is a tiny CPU the size of a fingernail-sell at around NT$10,000 a piece. Compared to the high value of the computer chips, the basic material cost is next to nothing. Microsoft produces something even more intangible-products of knowledge and the imagination-computer software programs. Strictly speaking, Microsoft products all are immaterial. But, Microsoft is not just the most profitable company in history and one of the world's fastest growing companies, its Chairman, Bill Gates, easily became the world's youngest tycoon.

That these two companies' stock values could surpass the stock value of the big three automakers portends an important concept: the wealth created from knowledge has already surpassed the wealth created from traditional manufacturing. Thus, in 1997, Intel's Chairman, Mr. Andrew Grove, was chosen to be *Time* magazine's Man of the Year, defeating such personages as Diana, Princess of Wales, and Dr. Ian Wilmut who successfully cloned a mammal for the first time, a sheep named Dolly. Fraught with natural disasters, human tragedies and epidemics, the year 1997 left an indelible impression. And, yet, the astounding success of this godfather of the computer chip industry offers us proof that a new wealth-creating system has been born, and that this is instigating a new quiet revolution around the world.

Taiwan cannot stand alone in this new wave of economic change. According to a report in *Asia Wealth Club* magazine, despite the sweeping losses brought by East Asia's financial crisis, the number of tycoons from Taiwan on their list of East Asia's one hundred wealthiest tycoons has increased.

It is noteworthy that the rise of the hi-tech industry brought along the new rich and fortunate. New hi-tech companies, like Asust and Taiwan Semiconductor Manufacturing Company (TSMC), display surprisingly vigorous growth and abundant profits that by far outstrip anything possible by traditional enterprises. TSMC, for example, was set up just ten years ago to make semiconductors. Its present stock market value stands at NT$485.5 billion, surpassing that of Cathay Life Insurance Co., Ltd. at NT$483.6 billion. It has the largest market value for listed companies on the domestic stock market. This kind of success by a hi-tech company confirms that depending on knowledge rather than more tangible resources to amass wealth is the new approach to create wealth. At the same time, it is causing a gradual change in our value concepts: even without a prestigious family background and capital conditions, anyone with the requisite training, talent and intelligence can become an outstanding success.

Wealth-creating System, from the Agricultural Age, to the Industrial Age, and on to the Network Age

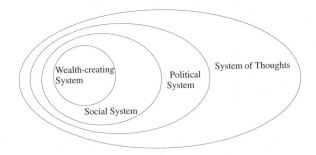

Now when we look back on changes and developments in human history, we can easily find that the initial starting point of every known civilization has been the establishment and completion of a wealth-creating system.

Several thousand years ago, our forefathers developed agriculture in the Yellow River basin. That is, they took up cultivating the soil as their means of creating wealth and ceased leading the nomadic life of following the water and green pastures. People began to live permanently around arable lands, forming hamlets, which grew into farming villages, and thus gradually forming a social system. This form of society is what we call an Agricultural Society.

As these farming villages became more numerous, how could disputes between villages be resolved? Who could judge who was right and wrong? According to what standards? In response to the evolving needs of the social system, political arrangements were set up to settle all sorts of quarrels and disputes that arose in the social system. As the political system gradually matured, a system of thought comprised of heaven, earth, emperor, personal relatives and teacher began to take shape. Thus, a fairly well-rounded civilization was formed. From this pattern of development, we get a clear idea of how every early civilization formed and took shape: they all sprang from well-established wealth-creating systems.

By the end of the eighteenth century, Newton's discovery of the laws of gravitation and Watt's invention of the steam engine had spawned the Industrial Revolution in England and human history had entered a new stage.

The greatest effect that the Industrial Revolution

exerted on humanity lay in changing the basic system of creating wealth. In the past, our creation of wealth was based on planting and cultivating the soil. After the Industrial Revolution, we began to depend on mechanized mass production systems to create wealth. As the large factories purchased and installed heavy machines and equipment, a dramatic change occurred in society: people became mobile. Instead of remaining in the same village for generations, they started to move to the places with the best jobs. In general, they moved from the countryside to city, and changed the political system in the process.

At the beginning of the twentieth century, our first political revolution led to a new democratic system, which changed the development of Chinese history. At around that time, in fact, many countries experienced political revolutions. Why? It was because the changes brought about by the new wealth-creating system of Industrial Revolution were global in extent. The mass production system led to changes in social structures around the world. This led to inevitable changes in political systems, including large, dramatic changes in the system of human thought.

This is why during the Agricultural Age there was

neither communism, nor capitalism. New systems of thought arose to accommodate changes in new social systems. Nowadays, in an age of high level development of computer technology, we stand astride a wave heralding the tide of an entirely new wealth-creating system.

Waves of Civilization

In his book, *The Third Wave*, Dr. Alvin Toffler discusses what he calls the waves of civilization. He divides human history roughly into three main ages:

1. Age of Agricultural civilization: using arable land to create wealth.

The most powerful people during the Agricultural Age are the landlords, not just because they hold the land, but because they hold the productive, arable land.

2. Age of industrial civilization: using capital to create wealth.

Next comes the era of creating wealth from capital. The most powerful people during this age are capitalists who operate factories and businesses to create lots of wealth.

3. Age of Network civilization: using knowledge to create wealth.

By 1980, people had already started to initiate the third civilization, the so-called "third wave." This is the new civilization based on using knowledge to create wealth. Starting around 1980, we witnessed the gradual appearance of people creating wealth from knowledge. By 1996, the fortune created through the wealth-creating system of the Network Age began to surpass the wealth-creating system of the old Industrial Age system made.

What is the new wealth-creating system?

How are we to create wealth from knowledge?

We are facing a brand new system for creating wealth (effective utilization of resources), a new means of creating wealth. Before attempting to understand this new wealth-creating system, we must first understand what is meant by the expression " wealth-creating."

At first sight, people commonly think wealth-creating just means a "way of making money." As a matter of fact, making money is just one activity within the total concept of a wealth-creating system. The simplest explanation of the wealth-creating system is the efficient utilization of resources. The essential element of any viable system of creating wealth is structures that will facilitate the efficient utilization of resources. What do we mean by "resources?" Generally speaking, there are two basic kinds of resources: human (manpower) resources, and natural resources.

Each one of us is a human resource. The term 'natural resources' encompasses virtually everything else in our environment including minerals, wood, and water.

To exploit resources means to make the most out of them, human and natural alike. Thus, the most important changes in any age will consist of the continuous refinement and improvement in the effective utilization of resources towards their productive end.

I recently read a report on the production of paper clips written about one hundred years ago, a century after the start of the Industrial Revolution. At that time, when a blacksmith wanted to make a paper clip, he had to grip a tiny strip of iron, fire it until it was red hot, strike it with his hammer, cool it, reheat it, then strike it again. He had to repeat this process many times. Consequently, at the time, it took a skilled blacksmith about two days to make one paper clip. For this reason, paper clips were a precious commodity in those days. Only the well-to-do and royalty could afford to use paper clips.

After the Industrial Revolution, the smelting furnace was invented, which made it possible to smelt vast quantities of high quality steel. Afterwards, molten steel could be poured into molds to make rolls of steel wire for producing paper clips. With this new technology a century ago a twenty-man production line could produce 4,800 paper clips per day. This little example gives a good indication of the vast difference in productivity between the Agricultural Society and Industrial Society, and of the difference in their respective means of resource utilization. Whereas a traditional, Agricultural Age blacksmith might make half of one paper clip in a day, his Industrial Age counterpart would make 240 paper clips in that same day (based on 20 workers producing 4,800 paper clips per day). In addition, the Industrial Age introduced a great simplification of the production technology.

This is to say that the same person can easily increase his production by dozens or hundreds of times solely because of effective use of human resources. This also means that the same person, after adopting a different method, could increase productivity, and consequently make much more money.

Two years ago, I read yet another report about machine production of paper clips. Present day machines can produce four paper clips per second. The new machine spews out new paper clips as fast as a machine gun fires bullets. One such machine can produce up to 330,000 paper clips in a single day.

Thus, we can see that the change in wealth-creating system is built on the development of technology. The worker who once made half of a paper clip per day, and later 240 paper clips per day, now can make 300,000 in that time. This sort of increase in productivity illustrates what we mean by the expression "creating wealth." At the same time, these advances benefit everybody. Cheap, easily obtainable paper clips-and thousands of other similar implements used in daily life-make our lives immeasurably more convenient than could have been hoped for in the past.

The same principle holds for natural resources. In the past, if a farmer struck oil in his rice paddy, it would have been considered bad luck. He would have had to pray to his lucky stars the oil would recede, because there was no market for oil in those days. Afterwards, petroleum became as precious as gold. In fact, it is called "black gold." If a farmer were to strike oil nowadays, he would regard it as a genuine blessing from heaven. Therefore, I always maintain that effective use of resources leads to the creation of wealth.

It is important to bear in mind that the systems for creating wealth that we are discussing today are standard, normal approaches to creating wealth. They are in no way involved in taking advantage of (robbing) others: we should understand the sources for creating wealth in any given context or situation in order to know how to go about creating wealth. This does not require coming up with hype or tricks.

Using Knowledge to Utilize Resources Even More Effectively

Simply stated, the new wealth-creating system is based on using knowledge to utilize resources even more effectively. If you can use knowledge in place of actual physical resources, you can start to earn money.

Let's look at a very simple example. Say that today we want to post a letter. We want to send it from Taipei to Shanghai. In order to do so, we must first write the letter, thus we will need a few sheets of factory made stationery. Having finished writing the letter, we will need to seal it into an envelope, so we will also need to have some factory made envelopes. We will next put the letter into the envelope, seal it, address it, and attach a stamp. Our stamp will come from a specially authorized factory. Now we will set off for a special Post Office and mail the letter. A series of postal workers will then load and unload the letter on a series of vehicles-trucks, trains, boats, planes, and even bicycles-in order to deliver it to Shanghai. After the letter reaches the Shanghai post office, it will be sorted and a mailman will deliver it to the address shown. At last, the letter will be in the hands of its intended receiver. He or she will read it and feel moved by this message from afar. But, by now one week has passed since it was written-it is read long after it was written.

This simple example gives an indication of how much effort is made and how many resources are utilized just to deliver a letter (expressing the feelings in a man's or woman's heart) into the hands of its intended reader.

Nowadays people often write each other by fax. If both parties have fax machines, the fax letter can be transmitted and be in the receiver's hands within two minutes time. It is hard to imagine how many resources are saved by sending a letter by fax rather than by the postal service. Because of all the advantages of time, money and resource savings, the inventor of the fax machine became a very wealthy man.

When fax machines were just starting to become popular, something funny happened to me. A friend of mine was stirred to purchase a fax machine as soon as he heard of it. On the very first day, he excitedly attempted to fax a letter to me. He spent a lot of time repeatedly trying to send the fax, but try as he might he just couldn't transmit the paper to me. Finally, he gave me a call. When I heard his voice at the other end, I immediately told him, "I got your fax. It's very sharp and clear." Greatly surprised, he replied, "How can that be? The original letter is still here in my fax machine. How could you have received it?"

It was a pretty funny situation. At first, most people assumed that the fax machine operated like ordinary mail: the same letter that is sent out is received at the other end. Naturally, by now, everyone knows that fax machines transmit messages by scanning the original paper with an electronic optical device and converting the images on the page into electronic data, which then passes through the telephone line to the receiving fax machine. The receiving fax machine then translates the electronic data back into the original images and makes a printout. This process marks an epochal advance over the traditional processes involved in delivering a letter.

We weren't quite fully satisfied with the fax machine, however: it still had to print out the message, and we still had to keep the paper. What we want most of the time, however, is the message, not the paper.

As personal computers became widely used, people started to wonder how data might be transmitted from computer to computer. This is why the Internet was so universally welcomed when it became more and more widely available, particularly because it offered a medium for sending E-mail (electronic mail). Not only can you send messages to people anywhere in the world in less than one second, the receiver can decide whether to store or delete the message at the press of a key. Developments of this sort can, of course, earn considerable wealth. Why, you may ask. These developments are the result of using knowledge to utilize resources even more effectively.

Consequently, the most basic principle of the new wealth-creating system is to replace traditional physical resources with knowledge. To better understand this idea of replacing traditional resources with knowledge, let us consider another example.

A new service has appeared in America called "phone pizza." Pizza is new to most people in Taiwan and China. What is unique about pizza is that people can adjust the flavor to their taste by choosing from among the various toppings offered, including sausage, pepperoni, beef, ham, anchovy, tomato, pepper, mushroom, and various cheeses. Nowadays, even Mexican, Chinese, vegetarian, and smoked chicken pizzas are available. The infinite variety of pizza flavors guarantee that they will become popular around the world. But, as with all sorts of foods, it takes considerable effort to go out for pizza. First, you have to get suitably attired and drive to a pizza parlor. Then, you have to park the car, enter the parlor, find a table and wait for the waitress to come and take your order. Oh, it's not easy to decide on which flavor to order. After that, you have to wait for the pizza to be prepared and baked. Finally, after twenty to thirty minutes, a piping hot pizza appears on your table.

Now stop and think for a minute and consider the entire investment involved in going out to eat a pizza. It is really quite large. You need a car, and a reasonably close restaurant. And, as to the restaurant, besides the standard furnishings, it needs to have cooks and waitresses, as well as expensive utilities. All these costs are borne by the customer. Thus, the capital involved in making and consuming pizza becomes very high indeed!

This high overhead led some people to think up the idea of phone pizza service: if you want to eat a pizza, you just need to make a call and a pizza will be delivered to your home in thirty minutes. By ordering pizza in this way, you needn't change clothes, get into your car and drive, and the restaurant needn't open a pizza parlor. It just needs a small place for a counter, a kitchen, some cooks and a clerk. The restaurateur can save much capital overhead, and the customers can save much effort, time and money. Much is saved, and the result of this savings in basic resources is good, convenient service. No matter where you are, you can have a piping hot pizza delivered to you within thirty minutes of placing your order. If your pizza is brought to you over one minute late, you don't have to pay for it!

It is relatively easy to provide quick pizza delivery service in Taipei and Beijing, because these are closely knit cities. People who live farther apart in places like the United States and Canada, often live over 30 minutes from a pizza shop, not to mention the time it takes to order, cook and deliver a pizza. In addition, the pizzas have to arrive freshly cooked and piping hot with the correct toppings. How could the pizza shops manage to solve the problem of providing on-time delivery?

The original solution was to install a pizza kitchen inside the back of a large truck and stock it fully with pizza crusts and ingredients. The pizza company then would deploy an army of several hundred such trucks around metropolitan areas to patrol the freeways. Whenever a pizza order was received by central operators, an order would be conveyed by a mobile phone to the truck nearest the customer's location. The cooks on board the truck would then set to work making the pizza to order as it proceeded toward the customer's location. They thus innovated a way to deliver truly fresh cooked, piping hot pizzas, made to order, directly to their customers' doorsteps easily within thirty minutes.

Nowadays, they even offer interstate delivery! Just think. In the not so distant past, you had to have a restaurant in the vicinity, you had to drive there, and the restaurant had to have a parking lot and so many other materials, equipment and personnel. There was an expenditure of many resources, but what was the basic reason for going to a pizza parlor? Just to eat something hot and delicious that you had specially ordered. Your main purpose is to eat a delicious pizza. Just think how much time and resources might be saved if people put their heads together to come up with ways to use the knowledge and technology at hand to serve pizza in more and more efficient ways. This case shows the secret to creating more wealth and this is what I call the new wealth-creating system.

The Concept of Human Resources

People are the most important link in the new wealth-creating system. They must be appreciated as the most important because human knowledge exists primarily in their minds, and the most precious resource in the new wealth-creating system precisely is knowledge.

What is knowledge?

Knowledge is information processed by logical thinking.

We all know that newspapers provide information. As a reader absorbs information from a paper, he processes it according to his prior knowledge and thought. In this way, the reader can transform the information he obtains into an article or even a book. This article and book then can become knowledge which eventually can become wealth. Knowledge plus application is technology. At a higher level, knowledge develops into wisdom.

What does the word "wisdom" mean? When we say that a certain person is wise, we want to imply that he is learned--he possesses a wide range of knowledge--but also that he is highly creative. Thus, according to this definition, wisdom includes knowledge plus creativity.

What is inventiveness? What is genuine creativity? They are the result of having both

Knowledge + Creativity

=Computer Software Program

=High Profit

=Knowledge creates wealth

=Trend

THINK

IDEA

BRAIN

wisdom and application. In this sense, inventiveness and genuine creativity consist of knowledge and creativity, plus application. At present, none of the important tools used to create wealth can be utilized apart from knowledge: they all contain some portion of knowledge.

Knowledge = Information + Logical Thinking

Wisdom = Knowledge + Creativity

Technology = Knowledge + Application

= Information + Logical Thinking + Application

Genuine Creativity and Inventiveness = Wisdom +

Application = Knowledge + Creativity + Application Method

According to this view, hi-tech industries are industries that contain a relatively larger portion of knowledge.

My company makes calculators. Thus, I am well aware that the process of making a calculator is no more complicated or difficult than that of making a bucket. While I know how to make calculators, I don't know how to make buckets. That is because the manufacturing processes are different. On the other hand, even though a calculator is easier to make than a bucket, a calculator carries a higher price tag than a bucket because its knowledge component is greater. Whether or not a product is hi-tech, whether or not it has a high price tag, depends, not just on the difficulty of the production process, but on the amount and degree of the knowledge.

Knowledge is produced in the human mind, because knowledge is a product of information processed through logical thinking. Computers are powerful computing devices, but no computer can think. No computer can produce knowledge. Only the human mind can think and produce knowledge. Therefore, human beings are the most precious resource in the new wealth-creating system. In the coming age, humans will be the most precious resource of all.

In the Agricultural Age, people cultivated arable land to create wealth. For this reason, landlords with arable lands possessed the most wealth in society. At the same time, tenant farmers were little better than farm slaves. These were indentured servants, bound to the land. They were paid according to how much they harvested in a given year. In those days, common people were just regarded as a sort of labor power, unimportant as individuals. Even today, people in many countries, in many societies, are paid according to the standard, "what a man sows, is what he will harvest." While tables, slide projectors and other equipment are considered assets in financial reports, human labor is not even figured into the tally.

In the new wealth-creating system, however, human talent is a real asset because wealth is now created by human knowledge and intelligence. Thus, Intel and Microsoft are two new style companies that were established by two outstanding leaders. The far-sighted wisdom of these two men defeated the capitalistic imperialism of the big three American automakers. This provides a good example of using knowledge to create wealth.

Natural Utilization of Natural Resources

Effective utilization of natural resources is another element of creating wealth.

At present, our use of natural resources takes forms like cutting down trees, pulverizing them, heating them, burning them, and the like. The way we exploit natural resources tends to be highly destructive and wasteful. We are very destructive in the way we go about putting up a house: we first clear and level the site, then we dig the foundation, and finally we build the structure out of tiles and steel-reinforced cement. Thus, the process of constructing a house involves a whole cycle of destruction.

In the future, we will have new technology that will give us softer, more natural ways to utilize our natural resources. Such relatively nondestructive means will be essential elements of our future ways of creating wealth. For example, nowadays we simply turn on the air-conditioner on a hot summer day-and waste a lot of electricity in the process. If we can find efficient natural ways to obtain solar power, wind power, or other forms of power, or if we can find alternative ways to obtain cool air, we will be able to save energy and create a lot of wealth.

How to Establish the New Wealth-creating System?

In most things, the principle "easier said than done" holds true.

Of course, the problem of setting up a new wealth-creating system is not a piece of cake. On the other hand, it is not as difficult as it may appear.

In this effort, it is essential that we understand the special characteristics of the new wealth-creating system, that we use science and technology to their utmost, and that we suitably modify our rigid, conservative and traditional management concepts along with changes in the system.

Setting up a Computers and Telecommunications Infrastructure

The first thing that should be done when setting up a new wealth-creating system is to establish a computer and communications infrastructure.

A computer is not a brain; it is a tool that manages and stores information. Let's take consulting the dictionary, for example. A good dictionary is quite a thick book. Some of the words in it are hard to look up, while others are easy. Research has been conducted on the time expended in looking up words: it takes about 12 seconds to look up a word in an English dictionary, whereas it takes just one second to look up the same word using a computer or an electronic dictionary.

This example illustrates the advantage of the new wealth-creating system: while both the old and the new methods and tools obtain the same result, the time expended using the old way is twelve times longer than the time expended using the new way. This saving in time expended indicates a related saving in capital.

Nowadays, with recent advances in software technology, whenever you encounter a new foreign word on the computer screen, you just need to mark the word, cue the computer dictionary with your mouse, and then the computer will translate the word automatically for you-in less than one second!

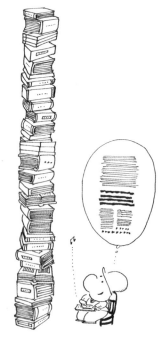

This example illustrates the far-reaching ability of contemporary computers to manage data. At the same time, contemporary computers can store large quantities of information. The notebook computer that I always use has a 2-gigabyte memory capacity. If I were to transfer 2 gigabytes of data to a paper hard copy, I would need 2 million sheets of paper to print out everything contained on the tiny hard disk. Just imagine how many books I would need to accommodate 2 million pages. If each book had 200 pages, I would need to use ten thousand books-about the number of books a bookstore keeps in stock. Just think: so much data can fit onto one tiny hard disk. This should give you some idea of how far our ability to obtain and store information has advanced. In the past, even if you had space to store ten thousand books, without a computer, how could you find any certain book or piece of information that you wanted from those ten thousand? In fact, even if a person has just five hundred books, he might have trouble finding the book he wants. Therefore, it helps to have a high-speed computer to store and manage data.

Building up Infrastructure of Telecommunications

What is the function of telecommunications? Telecommunications equipment provides ways to transmit messages and information.

In the past, it was not easy to contact other people. If you tried to make contact by mail, the letter you wrote might take a week, or even a month, to reach the other person. If you wanted to locate another person, you might possibly have been unable to find him. Nowadays, if we know a person's pager number or mobile phone number he just can't escape. You definitely can track him down. The contact you need to make, or the business you need to transact, needn't be delayed anymore. This is telecommunications: ways to transmit messages and information.

One important function of the human mind is processing knowledge. At the same time, people should make appropriate use of computers to process information. Knowledge consists of information processed through logical thinking; we use our minds to think over and process knowledge. By making appropriate use of telecommunications equipment, we can greatly speed up the flow and exchange of information and knowledge. In this way, the possibility of obtaining knowledge to create new wealth will develop faster and faster.

Establishing Society's Information Network

The next step is to set up society's information network. To date, all of our methods for obtaining information have been essentially on-receipt. Take the newspaper delivered to our door when we wake up in the morning, for example: its contents are all pre-edited. When we turn on the television, we have to watch programs that have been prearranged by station managers for us to see. All the books we purchase in the bookstore are prearranged and edited long before we ever get to see them. There is no way we can access them before they are arranged and edited. Thus, we can say that we live in a receptive society and that our methods for obtaining information have been, essentially, on-receipt.

In the future, information will pass freely through the Internet, and receivers will be in a better position to actively select what they receive. Be aware that telecommunications and the network are not the same thing: telecommunications essentially consist of communications between two parties. For example, when I call someone on the phone, the communications lie in the speech between my counterpart and I. The network, consequently, adds an important function to telecommunications: the network can access many data banks through telecommunications wires. If person 'A' were to input a certain command to obtain certain data, then, with the network's rapid transmission and processing of the command, every relevant data bank would be contacted in short order to obtain precisely the data that is being requested.

Let's say, today, I want to find a certain person for a job. Besides being a Mandarin speaker, this person has to speak Cantonese, Japanese and English, as well. How can I find such a person? In the past, looking for such a person would have been like looking for a needle in a haystack. If we were to add the condition that the person also must be between the ages of 25 and 30, the search would be even more difficult. Nowadays, however, among the information stored on the network are several personnel information banks: you can send out a message stating the job qualifications and specifications, and these data banks will respond with resumes of qualified job-seekers.

Thus, it is very important to establish an information network and data banks. As we approach the new wealth-creating system we will want, not just computer and telecommunications hardware equipment, but also an information network from which we can actively select the information.

Generally speaking, a bookstore that carries thirty thousand books is considered to be quite well stocked. Future bookstores could offer six to ten million books. Just think. In that case, how could anyone track down the book he or she wants? With the exception of providing an active online selection on a network, no bookstore could possibly display anything close to six million books. Even if we were talking about a library, and the collection held six million books, how many personnel would be required to track down the book you want? But, if you have computer access, you won't need anybody to help you search for the book. You will be able to go online and access a network to conduct your own search for the book you want.

Setting up Society's Knowledge Banks

We always say that this is an age of knowledge

explosion. This adage is really true. Our ancestors only had to read the Four Books and the Five Classics-just nine books in total. By contrast, a modern bookstore might carry several tens of thousands of titles. That's one of the reasons why we call this the knowledge explosion age.

But, this is also an age of insufficient knowledge: we often don't have the knowledge we would like to have, we often can't find the books we'd like to find.

Therefore-think carefully-why do we still call this a knowledge explosion age? Definitely, this description refers to the excess of information available. The reason why this proliferation of knowledge is called an explosion is that we still tend to use traditional methods to manage and process knowledge; that is why we can't find the books we want or learn the things we want to learn. We just feel that there are too many books out there, so many that we can't possibly obtain the information we need or want. This is what is really meant by the expression "knowledge explosion." If we were to set up a knowledge bank, however, and thus no longer be dependent on traditional books, whenever we had a question we could simply "ask the books" by consulting a knowledge bank.

A few days ago my son asked me, "Dad, why is gold, golden?" I tried to think of the reason why gold is gold-colored, but I couldn't. I had never entertained this question before. Nothing in the world has quite the same color as gold. How many books would you have to consult to obtain the answer to this question? Most people would be unable to track down the answer to this question. But, if we had "knowledge on demand," we could just input this question online and let the computer retrieve the answer from the knowledge bank. Our computer would actively seek the answer to your question in the sea of knowledge. Even if the computer couldn't find the answer out there that would be right, it could post the question in a general public knowledge bank. People who knew the answer then could reply to us over the network. At the same time, the proposed answer would be incorporated in the appropriate section of the knowledge bank. In this way, all knowledge would tend to increase greatly and the network would offer "knowledge on demand" service.

When I first heard about this, it sounded like someone's fantasy. But, the Internet has grown and developed significantly over the past several years and already provides access to knowledge banks that are in the initial stages of development. As computer technology develops further, these knowledge banks will become better. Still, we might come to feel that the available knowledge still isn't sufficient and that it isn't in fact exploding.

Knowledge is very important and essential for us. We can use it to create wealth, so increasing knowledge is necessary. The most convenient and efficient way to increase knowledge is through a knowledge bank. So, besides the establishment of computer and communications equipment, we have to set up information banks and knowledge banks as well.

Retraining Engineering

Whenever we talk about technology, the most difficult part of this subject is people.

In 1973, I was serving as a president in an electronic calculator company. Once during that time, I represented the industry in a debate. The debate topic was, "What is better, the electronic calculator or the abacus?" The main point of the debate was whether it was better for people to use calculators or abaci?

To hold a debate on this topic nowadays of course would seem like a joke. At that time, however, it was an important, controversial topic. The opposing team, composed mostly of elderly math teachers, spoke first.

They argued that using calculators causes our minds to grow dull. If people today were to use calculators all the time, they would lose the

ability to calculate by themselves. I countered that most American scientists and engineers use electronic calculators. By 1969, they had already sent men to the moon. Can we possibly call them dull or stupid?

The debate wrangled back and forth for quite a while. Finally, one elderly teacher stood up anxiously and heatedly "pointed out" to us in

a patronizing manner, "Supposing there was a catastrophe and no more calculators were left in the world, how would you be able to calculate?" At that time, we were in our twenties; full of youthful ardor, we couldn't help but stand up and reply, "Teacher, according to your logic, we should quickly leave this place and go off to learn how to start a fire by striking flint over kindling. Otherwise, if the world suddenly were to have no more matches or cigarette lighters, we'd be unable to cook food!"

Generally speaking, people often can't help feeling somewhat prejudiced against new technology. This doesn't mean that they actively resist new technology, however; it's just a subtle sense of insecurity that they feel in the face of change.

When Galileo observed with his telescope that the earth revolves about the sun, he issued a report announcing that the old view that the sun revolves about the earth was wrong. Even though it was true that the earth orbited the sun then as it does today, the church dominated the entire society in those days, and, to the church, Galileo's report was as heretical as it was unreasonable: how could it be that the vast earth revolves around the sun? The church council then placed Galileo under house arrest to think things over. He was not released until he eventually recanted and admitted that the sun revolves around the earth, not vice versa.

Galileo was a scientist. When he was placed under house arrest, he said, "There is no way out: even if you lock me up, it will remain true that the earth revolves around the sun."

Many human events transpire just as described in this story of Galileo. There hasn't been any major change in human nature down to the present day. However, there is one lesson to be learned in this: we should be receptive to new technology.

We should learn to think of new technology as a blessing of accumulated knowledge. Modern technology brings great improvements to our lives, without necessarily destroying the original beauty of our lives. Nowadays, even though we can contact our friends by telephone, this does not prevent us from going out to pay them a visit, as before. Nowadays, even though there are many convenient fast food services, we are not prevented from going to a fine restaurant to enjoy a gourmet meal.

Technology has been a real blessing to us. If at

2:00 a.m. on a snowy night, we suddenly want to eat some noodles, what do we do? Most likely, we will have some instant noodles on the shelf at home.

We earnestly accept new technology because it is fundamentally a blessing. It does not deprive us of what we now possess. People in the past, however, sometimes misunderstood technology. For example, people thought that if we were to use calculators we would be deprived of something else that was important. In fact, this was not true. Instead, the new technology brought along a lot of benefits. Therefore, a retraining project is badly needed in the new wealth-creating system. We need to retrain ourselves and society to accept new technologies with a healthy receptive attitude.

Nowadays, many children and young people are learning to use computers, so people tend to think that computers are just for kids. Does this mean that older people can't learn to use computers? Not at all. Whether or not one can learn to use a computer is not a matter of age. Seniors can learn computer just as young people can.

Recently, it has become popular in Taiwan for elderly men and women to learn how to use computers. Many government and social units actively encourage seniors to learn about them. I saw with my own eyes a 79 year-old man eagerly learning how to go online and surf the Internet. He learned how to do this quite quickly and smoothly, in no small part because the steps for learning how to use computers are becoming easier. The mother of Acer president, Stan Shih, also participated in this activity, and not just because her son is the president of a major computer producer. In fact, "Acer Mama" was no different than thousands of other elderly ladies in the countryside. These elderly didn't know exactly what a computer was, but they need someone to teach them how to use one. And, most importantly, they didn't resist the trend. Generally speaking, they can master the art in a short time. For example, one 80 year-old lady had lived alone for a long time, ever since her children resided overseas. Her only pastime was playing Mahjong. But, it became ever more inconvenient for the old lady to go out to play. When her children returned to Taiwan for a visit, they understood her predicament and bought a simple, basic computer for her to use. Now this old lady happily plays Mahjong on her computer every day.

The development trend in technology now is for hi-tech products to be easier and more convenient to use. Take computers for example. A few years ago, one had to learn quite a few basic commands in order to operate a computer. Now, with the Windows platform you can use a mouse to move a cursor to command the computer to execute a function for you. In our society today, some people have grown up in the Agricultural Age, others have grown up in the Industrial Age; nonetheless, all of these people have the opportunity to transform themselves into people of the information civilization. Even seniors can be retrained to use new technology and put the new technology to work to create wealth for them. Because people are resources, people themselves have knowledge, and knowledge can be harnessed to create wealth, this is wealth-creating engineering.

Establishing a Software
(in the Broad Sense) Industry

In 1991, I went to China to invest in the software industry. Even though China had no software industry at the time, I judged that the computer software industry was the most suitable industry to develop in China. Why?

When I was in Shanghai that year, many students from university computer software departments worked as tour guides because there was no computer software industry to speak of, in China. In fact, computer software is a large-scale industry. In the United States, for example, there are now over two million software engineers. That comprises about one percent of the total population. And, this one percent of the population designed and manufactured products that earned a total of $110 trillion dollars in total sales revenues.

Let's consider the relative situation of the Chinese community. At present, there are Chinese software companies in China, Taiwan, and Hong Kong. How many people are employed in the industry in total? Supposing the number were one percent of the total population of the Chinese community, that would be an incredible twelve million. Suppose the number was one thousandth of the total population, there would be one million two hundred thousand. Regrettably, the number of people employed in the computer software industry does not even amount to one ten thousandth of the total population. In other words, far too few of us are employed in the computer software industry, and so we lag behind the United States in this respect. This figure also suggests that we don't yet have the ability to make big money in the software industry. Naturally, I am using the term "software" in the broad sense of the word, to include a broad range of products, including books, CD-ROMs, VCDs, record albums, etc. These all are forms of software and all have huge markets. They are all basic representative kinds of products that have the potential to create great wealth in the new wealth-creating system.

The Third Movement: Creating Taiwan's Second Economic Miracle

Over 2,500 years ago, the Greek philosopher Heraclitus said, "A man cannot step into the same river twice, for the waters are ever flowing on." In the stream of time, every person will change into another sort of person, just as the water that flows in a river will not be the same water as that which flowed there before.

Creating Taiwan's Second Economic Miracle

Our first economic miracle transformed us from an Agricultural Society into an Industrial Society, and allowed us to escape the grip of poverty to begin to enjoy a better life.

In anticipation of the second economic miracle, what can we do to prepare ourselves?

Most importantly, we must establish Taiwan's economic independence by creating a new wealth-creating system that suits Taiwan's advantages.

Economic Independence

For quite some time, the government hoped that local industry would not invest in China, but would continue to invest in the local economy as before. In fact, this attitude was not very reasonable.

If a certain industry could become stronger and more competitive by moving to China or Southeast Asia, then it would be right to let it go there. Our present situation is that, if several companies move their production out of Taiwan, and the government then steps in to prevent other companies in the same industry from leaving, then the companies that heed the government, or are otherwise compelled to stay, will suffer losses and perhaps go out of business.

Our kung-fu novels and movies often tell the story of a hero who cultivates his martial skills to a certain level, but who cannot break through to a yet higher level. To solve the problem, he would often give up his original skills and take up an entirely new approach in order to reach the highest possible level of realization. I think that Taiwan's industry will produce results like this under the influence of China's black hole effect. In other words, as China absorbs a large portion of the traditional industries that grew up in Taiwan over the past thirty years, Taiwan enterprises will have the opportunity to seek a new turning point and transform into something completely new.

Facing the new age, what we really want to do is to create and establish industries that will enjoy great advantageous in Taiwan. That is to say, if a certain industry wants to make profits, then it must definitely do so in Taiwan in order to enjoy an advantage. Then, we should use Taiwan's advantages to create an industry uniquely suited to Taiwan. Our enterprises could therefore develop sufficiently and earn rich profits in this environment, to the extent that they cannot be driven away. This is the correct way of doing things.

If we want to establish economic independence, our economy cannot rely too heavily on the United States, Japan, or China.

In the new age, we will want to create a new wealth-creating system that is advantageous to Taiwan. At present, the conditions for this new turning point are already in sight: that is, capital-intensive, technology-intensive and speed-intensive industries.

Take a close look, you will find that capital-intensity, technology-intensity and speed-intensity are all characteristics of the most profitable businesses in Taiwan.

Take a close look at the most profitable businesses in Taiwan, you will find that capital-intensity, technology-intensity and speed-intensity are all characteristics of them as well.

Capital-intensity

Taiwan has been accumulating capital for thirty

years. Most of it is in the form of cash. Even if the amount of Taiwan's foreign exchange reserves does not rank first in the world, the per capita foreign exchange reserves far exceeds that of any other country. This sort of capital advantage is a card that Taiwan can bring into play. In fact, some enterprises have begun to draw upon this unique advantage of capital-intensity.

Technology-intensity

By providing facilities like the Industrial Technology Research Institute (ITRI) and the Science-based Industrial Park we have nurtured many local technologists, as well as a huge brain gain from overseas. Taiwan now has a very high concentration of technologists, which facilitates the process of researching and developing new products.

Speed-intensity

In the past, when we first started to industrialize, Taiwan was still a very poor country. In those days, no matter the cost to price ratio, no matter the means of making a sale, we struggled to win every possible business contract. Consequently, factories sprang up everywhere. From the point of view of efficiency, our response time and speed of operations were relatively fast. But, our ad hoc style of doing business led to a measure of chaos in society and in law and order. The streets were jammed with vehicles of all sorts: from trucks and buses, and cabs and cars, to motorcycles and bicycles: -all fearlessly plugging ahead. Wherever there was an opening on the road, a vehicle would bore through. Many foreign visitors were amazed by Taiwan's traffic and feared it was an impossible situation. But, Taiwan business flourished under these conditions. This was our advantage.

Naturally, things are quite different today. In the age of hi-tech industry, we definitely must maintain our quick response time and speed of operations. But, we

Failing to know how to use our resources well is like thinking oil truck in a field is a farmer's bad luck.

must also develop rational procedures and regularize our management style to suit the ordered, highly efficient world of hi-tech operations: only with orderly, rational, and speedy procedures can we develop suitably to produce excellent quality, world-class hi-tech products.

Consequently, if we can combine the factors of capital-intensity, technology-intensity and speed-intensity, we will create a new turning point in Taiwan's economic development. Looking at the current development in Taiwan, we can see that the formation of Taiwan's new industries is built on the characteristics of capital-intensity, technology-intensity, and speed-intensity.

Now that we understand the concepts of capital-intensity, technology-intensity and speed-intensity, we should devote ourselves to finding workable ways to establish and operate them.

If we continue to develop business in Taiwan, how will we develop capital-intensive, technology-intensive and speed-intensive industries?

Developing Capital-intensity

When I speak of capital-intensity, this is not to suggest that every single enterprise must raise tens of billions of dollars to succeed. Capital-intensity comes about through cooperation and alliance, through enterprises pooling their resources and bringing together capital from various sources. They want to gather large-scale capital because the very the first condition for industries with capital intensity, technology intensity and speed intensity, is capital-intensity.

During the Agricultural Age, we generally ran our businesses on the self-scale. After entering the age of industrialization we began to run our businesses on the economical-scale, that is to say, the national scale. Thus, the large companies that started in the Industrial Age tended to come from large countries. The bigger the market in the country, the larger the company is.

Taiwan went from the Agricultural Age to the Industrial Age in a remarkably short time. Naturally, some people felt that the change was too fast. Throughout history, family enterprises had been the core of the national economy. Now the concept of capital markets began to be realized.

Taiwan's change into an industrial economy took place under favorable circumstances. Overseas Chinese in Southeast Asia generally haven't been so fortunate because they often encounter some big limitations.

I have a friend in Thailand who runs five restaurants there. Every one of his restaurants is profitable. I asked him, "With business so good, why don't you open some more restaurants?" He replied, "I can't open any more. Sons and sons-in-law, total just five." He still thought according to the self-scale of the

Agricultural Age. This had become his self-limitation.

Nowadays, people often think that the Network Age will allow a return to the idea of "small is beautiful" enterprises. In fact, this is not quite so, because in the Network Age everything proceeds on a global scale. Our transactions are all globally interconnected.

The reason why the total stock market value of Intel and Microsoft can surpass that of the big three American automakers is that they enjoy global scale capital-intensity. Just think, how such companies can sprout up and reach a global scale in such a short period of time! In the future world of the twenty-first century, companies will need to be even more capital-intensive in order to stay competitive. Therefore, no matter whether it's through mutual investment, cooperation or alliance, companies will need to reach the level of global scale capital-intensity in order to stay competitive with their competitors.

Developing Technology-intensity

Next, how are we to develop technology-intensity? Above, we defined technology as knowledge, plus the way to implement it.

- Technology = Knowledge + Application

Nowadays, it is extremely easy to manufacturer a PC. People claim you can assemble a PC right in your own garage. But, if you were to try to construct a bucket, well, I think that most people would be unable to do it. In terms of having a way to implement it, a bucket certainly is not easier to construct than a PC. We believe that a PC is hi-tech and has a higher market value than a bucket because a PC contains a larger component of knowledge than does a bucket.

To advance our discussion a little, let's consider what we mean by "knowledge."

Knowledge, by today's definition, is information processed through logical thinking. For example, when a body of fresh information is obtained, some experts will analyze it and reflect on its larger meaning to produce actual knowledge.

- Knowledge = Information + Logical Thinking

If we want to develop technology-intensive

industries, the first requirement is to focus on industries with a greater component of knowledge; the second requirement is to have teams of experts in 4 major technologies.

Every kind of industry has four basic kinds of technology: R&D technology (to develop new products), duplication technology (for mass production), management technology (for systematic management operations), and exchange technology (for sales and purchasing). Every kind of industry has to utilize these four main domains of technology. The greater the knowledge component in each of these four major technologies, the higher the value of the products.

Of course, we don't necessarily want to develop our own teams of experts in the four main domains of technology. We can borrow experts from other companies, while at the same time it is important to observe the extent to which other companies have technology-intensity.

Technology-intensive Industry

In the future, Taiwan will have to pursue all out

development of technology-intensive industries. According to my analysis of the present situation, there are three industries that deserve our attention in this regard.

(The Semiconductor Industry and Related Industries)

The most noteworthy industry in this regard is the semiconductor industry and related industries. The semiconductor industry is a very standard, government conceived industry.

In the late 1970s, an experimental IC (integrated circuit) factory was set up in Taiwan. After being managed and operated by some scholars trained overseas and the government for ten years, the project began to absorb large-scale capital in the late 1980s. This was necessary because the semiconductor industry requires a lot of capital. By 1990, this industry had become rated the most potential and highly educated industry in Taiwan.

In 1995, of Taiwan's US$8.1 billion dollars in trade surplus, some $2 billion was earned by the top five semiconductor factories. These figures illustrate everything we have been saying about capital-intensity, technology-intensity and speed-intensity in the semiconductor industry: the contribution of this industry to Taiwan's economic development has been immense.

(PCs, Mother Boards, Computer Peripherals, and Related Industries)

The 1996 earnings for Acer and manufacturers of PCs, motherboards, computer peripherals in addition to other related industries reached NT$27 billion dollars in total sales.   As everyone knows, these industries are all star industries in Taiwan. They are also perfect examples of industries that satisfy the conditions for capital-intensity, technology-intensity and speed-intensity.

(Notebook Computer and Related Industries)

In the past three years, other invading armies that broke through the front lines were notebook computers and related industries, which utilize the intensity in capital, technology and speed even more than the semiconductor industry. Bringing into play Japanese and Chinese expertise with making light, and miniature products, together with the existing computer industry as a foundation, our export value of notebook computers reached US$6 billion in 1996, ranking first in Taiwan in terms of unit export items. Moreover, the notebook computer is also the most expensive electronic product in terms of unit price. Today, the cost of two high capacity notebook computers approaches the price of one automobile.

At present, we can hold up these three industries as examples of industries that embrace capital-intensity, technology-intensity and speed-intensity in order to succeed. I believe that by using our active entrepreneurial spirit we can continue to develop new industries in Taiwan.

Developing Speed-intensity

Speed-intensity refers to what we usually call "enterprise acceleration."

How can an enterprise speed up? Anyone who drives a car knows what it means to speed up. But, how can an enterprise become a high-speed enterprise? This question is well worth exploring.

In order for an enterprise to speed up, it must speed up its operations. Speed-intensity does not mean that everything is rushed. What it does mean though is that an organization and system are streamlined so that operations speed up automatically. As this is obviously a large topic, we shall discuss it more fully in a separate chapter.

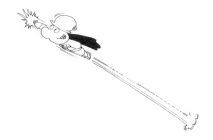

The Fourth Movement:
Enterprise Acceleration

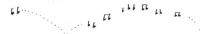

Time is one of the most important factors for modern hi-tech industries to succeed. No matter whether you are engaged in hi-tech industries or not the pursuit of speeding up an enterprise's operations is an urgent matter. Speeding up policy decisions, new product development, information flow, materials flow, cash-in, and other conditions are all aspects of enterprise acceleration.

Enterprise Acceleration

In the old days we had heavy industry and light industry. Heavy industry meant heavy investment and heavy products; light industry meant lighter investment and light products.

Now this classification has gone out of date. New industries like the semiconductor industry require more capital than the steel industry. So, now we have the hi-tech industry and the low-tech industry. The former is an industry that involves a higher level of knowledge and technology, while the latter implies a simple or mature industry.

Today this classification is becoming obsolete. The 486PC was no doubt a hi-tech product a few years ago. Even today, compared with many electronics products, the 486PC is still quite hi-tech, but it is already a fading low-tech product in the PC family. Now it is the Pentium II/III that are in great demand.

In this new hi-speed society, we have to classify industries into hi-speed and low-speed industries. Hi-speed industries are those that ride the tide of social trends; the industries that trail behind are low-tech industries. In the near future, we may see the birth of many so-called hi-speed enterprises; countries too will be classified into hi-speed countries and low-speed countries.

What is deemed a brand new computer today will be obsolete and sell for half its original price within a year. In no other industry is the situation so changeable: you purchased a new computer in January for US$2,000, and find that the same model costs just US$1,000 at year's end.

A stagnant year would result in the shutdown of large computer companies, including IBM and Compaq, because a loss incurred could run up to 50% at year's end. The meager annual profit margin of hi-tech industries is 5% at its best, therefore the impact

of a stagnant year on the industry is conceivably great.

Time has become a key factor in the hi-speed industry, in a hi-speed society everybody has to fight against time. I want to introduce the 5 principles by which to accelerate the speed of an enterprise. I call these the "5 Principles for Accelerating an Enterprise."

Today no matter whether you are engaged in the hi-tech industry or not, transforming your own business from low-speed into hi-speed is the only way to survive.

Acceleration Principle 1:
Decision-making Acceleration

When we drive on local streets, it is legal to make a u-turn if we've missed an exit. However, once we've missed an exit on the freeway we may have to continue driving for another 20 km or more before we can exit. In the same fashion, in a hi-speed society, slow decision-making procedures can make us miss some great opportunities. Thus, how to speed up the decision-making process is the key to success. How can we speed up our decision-making process?

a. Small Group Decision-making

A proverb says that, "the camel is a racing horse designed by a committee." Decision-making by groups may appear to be more democratic, but too many different opinions on the table will often blur the central topic, and synthesizing those opinions will waste much precious time. So, the first step to accelerate decision-making is to cut down the number of persons involved in the decision making process. The fewer the decision-makers that there are the better.

b. Base Decisions on the Latest Information

Today, our salary is 100 times that of the US$10 that we earned in the 1970s. Our income and consumption habits are very different from those of the old times of poverty and frugality. It is of course very hard to make decisions based on past experience, which does not mean experience has no value at all. What's more important is that we need to judge the circumstances based on the latest information.

c. Anytime, Anywhere Decision-making

Very often we consider decision making to be

something very serious. We think the decision-makers have to sit in a meeting room, think the problem over thoroughly, and then make a decision.

In fact, many of the most important decisions made in human history were made during simple conversations. Today's decision-maker may make his or her decision on the telephone, in the hallway, in a hotel, or, indeed, in any sort of unofficial occasion. Whenever there is the need to reach a conclusion, a decision can be made on the spur of the moment and be acted upon right away.

d.Quick Change

"You can't change your morning decision in the evening" was a guideline for a decision-maker or leader in the old Agricultural Society, in which the pace of life and the channels of communication were slow. But, today, as soon as one discovers a wrong decision or hits upon a better one, one should not just make us "change the morning decision in the evening," one should make us "change the morning decision in the morning." Decisions made at 09:00 am should be modified immediately upon receipt of new information even if it's just one hour later at 10:00 am. A decision is revisable, and the most critical thing is to correct it to match the latest status even after a wrong decision has been made.

The acceleration of decision-making is the most important key to enterprise acceleration. A decision-maker's decision made 1 or 2 days' earlier could save a whole enterprise one-month's effort, or more.

Acceleration Principle 2: New Product Acceleration

There are over 2 billion people in Asia engaged in the manufacturing business. Therefore, not only will you fail to make a profit, but you will also lose money if your product is similar to competitors.

"Innovate or Lose" is the new concept recently brought up by Mr. Ohmae Kenichi, a Japanese strategist. With today's fierce competition, enterprises either innovate or lose. Without innovation, it is impossible for an enterprise to break even, not to mention make a profit. Enterprises must constantly turn out new products, because only new products can make a market unsaturated. In a world with an oversupply of everything, only new products make it possible for enterprises to enter an unsaturated state.

A new product starts from an idea, goes through development, marketing, and finally starts to generate sales and profit in the end. There are 4 important indices for timing new product development:

a. Time to Idea (TTI)

As noted above, 'I' (Idea) means the idea suggested; 'P' (Product) refers to product developed; 'M' (Market) refers to entering a market; and 'V' (Volume) means volume production.

The first index of new product acceleration is TTI (Time to Idea). Very often we bring out an idea and ask the development team to work on it day and night according to a very tight schedule. Very seldom do we notice that we actually could have brought up the idea days, weeks or even months earlier. Several days'

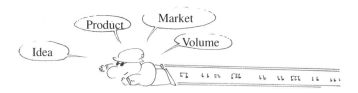

delay in the development schedule arouses serious concern, but not many people pay attention to TTI. If you come up with a creative idea earlier than anyone else, you are already in the lead.

b. Time to Product (TTP)

The second index is TTP (Time to Product), that is, to shorten the time between introduction of an idea and development of a new product. Besides utilizing concurrent engineering, in the future we plan to start using "relay development" to shorten time. Many factories have 3 shifts working on their production lines. This concept can be applied to new product development teams in order to fully utilize the 24 hours in a day. All things involve time. The greater your speed, the further your lead.

c. Time to Market (TTM)

The third index is TTM (Time to Market). This means shortening the time between completion of product development and the first shipment of a product to the market.

d. Time to Volume (TTV)

The fourth index is TTV (Time to Volume). After entering a market, a new product should be mass-produced in the shortest time possible, in order to maximize sales and profit.

Today, you made a new product. Probably, you were the first to develop the idea. Maybe there were delays in R&D, or in scheduling R&D, but you were too late to market. Maybe you were the first to enter a market, but this didn't guarantee you would make money. It's possible the new product could not be mass-produced. If you couldn't mass-produce the product then you couldn't make money.

Acceleration in the release of new products can be guaranteed only by following through TTI, TTP, TTM and TTV simultaneously.

Acceleration Principle 3:
Information Flow Acceleration

How do you speed up the flow of information within an organization? In the past, in countries with no freedom of speech, books had to undergo various levels of censorship, which often took up to a whole year. By the time the book was published, it was no longer in demand. The leader in world news, CNN, which came about in the 1980s, requires each reporter to present the news within ten minutes after gathering all the information. In contrast to the past when viewers learned about daytime occurrences from nighttime TV news, the flow of information has improved a great deal. This is the speeding up of the flow of information.

Then, how do you speed up the flow of information within an enterprise?

a. Using Computers

If I were asked by someone how to get to Kaohsiung (a port city in southern Taiwan) quickly from Taipei, I would say by airplane, which would be the fastest, or by train or by car driving at 120 km/hr. But if the person insisted on riding a bicycle, how could he get there quickly? Enterprises that are not using computers, but hope to accelerate the information flow are in this sort of situation. One who does not use a computer just can't imagine how weak his competitive position is when he faces other computer-savvy competitors.

The key to whether a company is computerized does not lie in whether there is a computer center or whether there are computers. Do the leaders - the chairman, the president use computers? That is the key factor when it comes to judging whether or not a company is computerized. If the boss does not use a computer, how could he fully understand the power and function of one?

b. Using Communications Equipment

The time has passed when one who goes abroad is isolated, or when things come to a stop just because a certain person is not in the office. The prevalence of modern telecommunications makes everyone in the world a neighbor. We have telephones, fax machines, pagers, cellular phones, E-mail, etc. by means of through we can contact anyone in a

Chairman

President

Director

Senior Manager

Section Manager

Staff

company anywhere, at any time.

c. Free Flow of Information

The organizational structure of an enterprise assigns special duties and powers to each of its various departments. This organizational structure should not become a filter that slows down the flow of information. Information inside an enterprise must flow freely, with the exception of confidential information. How do you achieve the free flow of information within a company? The most effective method is simultaneous reporting.

d. Simultaneous Reporting

A traditional reporting system filters through a chain of command - clerks reporting to section managers, section managers to department managers, department managers to senior managers, senior managers to vice presidents, and vice presidents to the company president. In the end, perhaps due to polite consideration or other reasons, the company president knows the least, and the chairman knows nothing.

The result of this traditional reporting system is that upper levels of management learn too little about a company too late. In today's large-scale companies, this can be dangerous since the most influential members of a company know the least, a great flaw in management.

For the past 6 years, we have implemented the "Simultaneous Reporting System." When a clerk reports to his or her section manager, he or she will also send an E-mail to relevant department managers, senior managers, vice presidents, company president, and even the Board. In this way, upper-level of management immediately knows what is happening on the ground level. The higher one's position, the more reports one receives.

In the past, every employee's results, including the security guard who does security inspections, are reported to the chairman. So, the chairman receives several thousand e-mails everyday. Is there an information overload? In my experience there isn't.

After the deployment of simultaneous reporting, all problems will resolve themselves. Everything is publicized, and nobody bullies anybody else, resulting in uplifted morale. Any problems raised will mostly resolve themselves immediately, which saves a lot of trouble for management.

This is a concept we mentioned before - in order to speed up the flow of information, we need to use computers and communications equipment to enable the information to circulate freely within an organization. Simultaneous reporting is the most effective method for making the "dead corners" disappear and utterly speeding up the flow of information.

One winter when one of our colleagues in Shanghai was taking a shower in the company shower room, the hot water stopped. He angrily sent an E-mail message to his manager to complain, and to all the managers in Taipei, even the company president and the Board. The Administration Manager of the Shanghai Company suggested that this "trivial" issue should have been reported only up to a certain level. Although we didn't point fingers at the manager, none of us thought we should stop any colleague from expressing his opinion, especially in a case like this. After all, having no hot water to rinse his soapy body on a freezing winter day with a temperature of around

0 degree centigrade was no trivial issue to him.

In the last six years, the Simultaneous Reporting System has accelerated the information flow inside the company tremendously. It has also helped to raise the morale of all company employees, improved the decision-making ability of middle management, and lubricated communication between different levels.

Acceleration Principle 4:
Material Flow Acceleration

As previously mentioned, a computer company which is not able to sell the stocked goods it acquired at the beginning of the year by the end of the year will certainly have to close. Therefore, it is vital for a modern enterprise to accelerate material flow. There are a few feasible ways to help use reach this goal.

a.   Information in Place of Inventory

The famous Japanese TOYOTA Company brought up the "Zero Inventory" concept. The essence of this concept is to precisely control material flow so that materials arrive at the production line on time, in order to cut down on inventory, with zero inventories as the goal. Some companies misunderstand the meaning of "zero inventory," and think that zero inventories means no spare materials in the warehouse and ask suppliers to accommodate. The low-price parts vendors are forced to keep inventory in their own warehouses, while the high-price parts vendors force you to pack your warehouse full. Thus, the company is constantly holding a huge volume of high-priced parts, while at the same time constantly waiting for low-priced parts. The proper way of managing inventory is to keep trace of it and use information in place of its dynamic in-flow.

Phone pizza, mentioned previously, is a good example of utilizing new technology to improve material flow. In fact, all businesses could find their own way to do this. Even companies that sell such low-priced goods as pizza could do so. How could we accelerate material flow if our enterprise did not use information to trace inventory and expedite the ordering of key components?

b. Credit in Place of Inventory

To a supplier, the worst thing that can happen isn't

extra requirements on quality or price but the cancellation of an order or refusal of delivery. Not owing any debts alone doesn't mean good credit: in the hi-speed era, nobody can foretell rises and falls in the market. Even world-class companies such as IBM and Compaq could not keep its promise to place a certain amount of orders to you. Therefore, you should always update your up-stream and down-stream suppliers with the latest information that orders may be increased or cut down so that you can have enough time to respond. This is what we deem as good credit. So, being honest to suppliers and telling them accurate information in time is the best way to reduce mutual losses and build up mutual trust. With this deep trust in mind, the contingent safety stock can be greatly reduced.

The best method is to use credit in place of tangible stock. Thus, the inflow of stock will be less, and the outflow will be faster.

c. Quality vs. Material Flow

Nowadays, you cannot talk about the price of materials, you must know that bad quality is the killer of material flow.

Many people have probably had the experience of buying a cheap component that failed you at a critical moment. Suppose all the work, production process and 99% of components are there waiting. All that is needed is a cheap component. If a bad quality component is implemented in this case, it could probably cause a company to go bankrupt.

You should always keep in mind that bad quality is the killer of material flow.

Quality is not only a cost issue, but also a key factor for company survival. A company with poor quality will not have a cost problem because there is no room for it to exist.

d. Zero Lead-time Age

I once wrote an article, "Zero Lead-time Age" (see appendix) in which I claimed that the greatest waste of a company was producing a product that didn't sell.

When a product does not sell, a company's decision-making will be affected. A company's best sales people will be assigned to sell a most un-sellable product, which absolutely wastes a lot of resources.

Thus, "Zero lead-time" is the best concept. This is to say that the most complete and latest information is essential to key parts, finished goods, and wholesalers. Suppose we notice that a wholesaler has sold 10 sets. We should then immediately arrange to produce 10 more sets. This can be likened to a water company's delivery of water. When a faucet is turned on, water runs out; when the faucet is turned off, water stops running. This reduces a lot of waste in the whole process from production to sales.

In the past, manufacturers produced and displayed computers in the store for customers to buy. Later on, some Americans came up with the new idea of "made-to-order." Those who came up with the new idea not only made a lot of money, but also caused a considerable revolution in the production and marketing of computers.

Acceleration Principle 5:
Cash-in Acceleration

a. Cash is the final product of a business

An enterprise is a system that creates wealth. The

basic raw material is cash, and the final product is also cash. The effectiveness of the enterprise is judged by the cash increment created by the system.

Many companies today play with their financial reports, gamble in the stock market, and engage in money games. They have lost the original essence of a company, which is to earn a profit through production and sales. The ability to cash in materials should be valued as much as the ability to earn a good profit.

b. Cash Inventory

Today a healthy enterprise should have extra money in the bank for emergency needs. Traditionally, extra money was called "idle money" because it was not being effectively utilized. I often jokingly say that, "idle money is better than no money." People finally realized how important cash inventory was when those countries without cash inventory all went bankrupt during the recent East Asian financial crisis.

You always have to keep in mind that cash inventory is more important than material inventory. Many painful cases caused by the East Asian financial crisis have showed us that this is an age of "no cash, no survival."

"Time" is becoming an even more precious resource in the hi-speed era. The president of Coca Cola once said, "Our fiercest competitor isn't Pepsi, but time." In Intel, the top level management changed the business adage "Time = money" to "Time = money2."

Every time I think about the importance of time to an enterprise, I recall a vivid scene in a western movie. On the western plains, John Wayne puts his gun that is still smoking back into his holster, then, looking down at the guy sprawled out in the dust, says, "This is the price of being slow!"

The Fifth Movement: Industry Transplantation

Industry transplantation is the best way for industries to move out. This is similar to when trees that can no longer grow well in their own forests are transplanted somewhere else.

Industries that upgrade involve upgrading to capital-intensity, technology-intensity and speed-intensity. In Taiwan, recently, quick development has made some industries unable to upgrade to capital-, technology-, and speed-intensive industries, so they have had to move out. The best way is industry transplantation. The question is how do we move an industry to another country? What problems should we pay the most attention to?

1. Split Process

The most widely seen model is "Split Process," which is also a Japanese's specialty.

An industrialized country transfers some portion of a manufacturing process of an industry to a developing country to take advantage of cheaper labor and cheaper natural resources in order to reduce total production cost. Or, they send semi-knocked-down (SKD) or completely-knocked-down (CKD) products to a developing country to assemble and sell locally in order to avoid the high tariff or trade barriers set by the developing country.

Through this Split Process, a developing country

can learn from an industrialized country some management techniques and production technologies. However, the disadvantage of this model is that key technologies are still in the hands of an industrialized country, the local people trained in a process cannot develop their own industry by themselves, and profit left for a developing country would be very limited. On the other hand, an industrialized country also has to do extra work to integrate the split production process both at home and abroad, and the extra effort and cost will very likely offset some of the benefits.

Not long ago, when we were transplanting industries, our government advocated a policy that enterprises keep their roots in Taiwan. When Wang Yung-ching decided to invest in Haicang (海滄), our government advised him to keep his roots in Taiwan. Mr. Wang then replied, "What if I remit the earned profits back to Taiwan? Does this move account for keeping my roots in Taiwan?"

As I delved deeper into analyzing the issue, I found that entrepreneurs and politicians are different in nature. For example, a politician representing the Chung-shan district of Taipei has to be very familiar with the people and the customs of his district. He is like a tree planted in a specific area. An entrepreneur, however, has to survive competition. He is like an animal running to and fro in a forest. Do to their different nature the animal-like entrepreneurs have problems understanding why the tree-like politicians always declare the need to "keep your roots planted in the same place." Let me cite another example. If a candidate for the legislature of the Shih-lin district is supported by the people in his district, he might be successfully elected. However, an entrepreneur, though supported by all the residents of the Shih-lin district, can not survive without orders. That is why the slogan of keeping one's roots in the same place was so conflicting for entrepreneurs.

According to the interpretations of some officials, to keep one's roots is to maintain Research & Development (R&D) in Taiwan while moving production. It sounds reasonable at first glance. However, all enterprises have their own competitive advantages - some are strong in marketing, some in R&D, and some in production. Most of these Taiwanese enterprises that need transplanting have a competitive edge in low cost. Basically, their R&D is relatively weak. What is the use of moving the stronger production abroad and keeping the relatively weak R&D in Taiwan, If integration problems are created. This method will not work. Therefore, split-process is not the best way to transplant an industry.

2. Purchase of Technology

Buying technology from industrialized countries is also a common practice for a developing country to raise the industrialization level. However, technologies are evolving themselves and improving day by day. Technology is not still water, but a running stream. We can buy a bucket of water, but not a stream. In buying a technology, if a developing country is unable to train a team of engineers who can immediately turn a technology into manufacturing products, both the purchased technology and the money will be wasted, especially since "technology" today doesn't merely mean "the ability to produce." Being able to make a product but not being able to mass-produce one is not "technology"; being able to mass-produce a product, but not being able to complete one is not "technology" either. True technology calls for making a product, mass -producing it in large quantity and competing in the market in the long term.

Although the model of Purchasing Technology is often on the table when industrialization is brought forth, looking around, we do not see many successful examples. Because developing countries usually cannot build their industries simply through Purchase of Technology, this trade often becomes a "one-shot deal." Thus this model is not the best one.

3. Industry Transplantation—The Shortcut to Industrialization

Now I would like to introduce another model, which is by far the best one. I have named it "Industry Transplantation." This is the shortcut to industrialization. Consider a forest with its various plants. When the natural conditions such as climate, soil, rainfall and temperature change, some plants will not be able to survive anymore. Moving those plants to another suitable location is the way to save them. This process is called "Transplantation."

By the same token, when a country's monthly wages rise from US$10 to US$1000 and per capital income increase from US$400 to US$15000 ~ 16000, the social environment and social values will change as well. Some industries may become unsuited for this environment, so they may have to be moved. This is why we need Industry Transplantation.

The question is - how do we proceed?

a. Judgment and Choice — Choosing the Strategic Industries

First, make sure the industry cannot survive in Taiwan and indeed needs to move out. Before you short-list the potential candidates, collect sufficient information and consult experts. Then pay a personal visit to those countries. "To see is to believe," and the top executives should visit these countries to understand local politics, culture, languages, laws, the government's efficiency, population, educational level, living standards, labor costs, public utilities, living conditions, and so on. This is the most effective way to find the right partner. Do not spend all your time in the country socializing at banquets, and never make any rash decisions under circumstances where one is not sober. This is dangerous and erroneous.

b. Matchmaking — Finding Suitable Partners and

Conditions

Matchmaking is finding the most suitable area and business partner.

One of the most important factors is to make decisions based on the nature of activities of your company. In the past, many of our small and medium enterprises made money by manufacturing. They found that land was increasingly profitable and they therefore developed blind faith in land investment. Unavoidable, many of them adopted the same approach while making investments in a foreign country with rough decisions to invest where land was either cheaper or had a good location.

Taiwan has rare land resources, so it is too costly for most residents to obtain land with a good location. On the other hand, South Asia and Mainland China have much more land than Taiwan. Therefore, we are likely to buy land when we first see it. However, it is wrong to believe that land is the only factor for decision-making.

c. Implementation

Transplantation of the upper, middle and lower

streams of an industry in one go is the key to transplantation. If one transfers partially, it becomes the "Split Process" again.

The first major step of transplantation is to integrate the upper, middle and lower stream industries. The lack of coordination will immediately cause problems.

For example, you are transplanting your badminton racket company to somewhere in Mainland China. You must make sure that your upper, middle and lower streams are all acting in accord with you. If your assembly units are all in Mainland China, but your raw materials are in Taiwan or Southeast Asia, then you will have save labor costs, but raise other costs.

(Ambassadors for Technology Transfer)

Industry transplantation is not simply moving enterprises. A company also needs to choose appropriate ambassadors for technology transfer to accompany its enterprises to a country.

According to our experience, the settlement of these expatriates and their families in to a new country is the most crucial and most difficult job. Perks, food, living conditions, medical care, education for employees' children, language, religion, entertainment, visa, etc., all of these have to be carefully arranged and resolved one by one. All of these minor issues could become key excuses for expatriates to quit.

If you are not well prepared in advance, only single people, the divorced, or the ones with marital problems will be willing to go. They will only solve short-term problems, which is not the total solution for a technology transfer. Because these people will not be able to concentrate on work, they will turn out to be a disorderly team. Consequently, the scheme will fail completely.

(The Nurturing of Local Talents)

Usually, industries move to another country because of lower labor costs. Many Taiwanese businessmen are puffed up with arrogance and treat local people as slaves, which is an unacceptable behavior.

I always say that poverty does not mean stupidity. Take Mainland China as an example. A person's poverty is caused by the social system instead of by his stupidity or incompetence. In fact, talent is everywhere waiting to be discovered, to be nurtured and to be respected. Only through the nurturing of local talent can a business develop roots locally.

(Mutual Trust)

Mutual trust is another key factor of industry transplantation.

You can find many people in Mainland China and South Asia searching for investors. When searching for suitable industries and sites to invest in, it is very common to encounter a situation where people tell you what you see is a terrific land, but pre-served for someone else and request your immediate decision to secure the land or something like that. Whenever I have faced such a situation, my answer has always been "you can go ahead and sell it". Obviously, their objective is to obtain your money, rather than to help you find the best investment.

Do not be controlled by land promotion tricks. You are looking for long-term investments, so mutual trust should be carefully established with written contracts. Few cases of deception happen in Taiwan because people get along better here. However, contracts are essential to protect your rights and interests in a foreign country.

Long-term Investment

Investments, whether made domestically or abroad, should be done on a long-term basis. Investment without a long-term plan can easily trap investors in a tight spot or dilemma. Cheap labor, cheap land, tax exemption, preferential interest rates, and GSP are all incentives that attract foreign investments, but investors should always regard them as a bonus. Investing in a new country is in essence launching a business there. It is wise to make sure that the new country is suitable for investment, before proceeding with a long-term plan.

The same rule applies to industry transplantation. First, make sure that the home country is no longer suitable for the industry before moving out so there will be no need for re-transplantation.

Once you decide on industry transplantation, you must make plans for long-term investments. Then, you will spend more time establishing communications and mutual understanding with local government officials, enterprises and employees, thus forming relationships for long-term mutual trust. Only then can industry transplantation succeed.

Industry transplantation like this will benefit both parties. Only when both sides benefit will cooperation last.

The Sixth Movement:
Preconditions for a Second Economic Miracle

If we want to create a second economic miracle in Taiwan, our enterprises will have to work hard, change their stance, and their direction, become capital-intensive, technology-intensive and speed-intensive industries, or serve as peripheral industries, satellite factories, or investors.

Japan's strategist, Ohmae Kenichi, has said, "Enterprises create wealth; the government distributes wealth." His statement contains one implicit precondition: these enterprises are already mature.

In the early days when we were forging our first economic miracle and the government hadn't provided guidance, we would have had fewer opportunities to succeed. Now that our enterprises have reached a definite scale and standard of operations, and we are at the beginning of our second economic miracle, our enterprises themselves have to stand in the batter's box and actively take their swings. So, the first thing they must do is to transform and change direction.

Nowadays, the cost to open a new factory in Mainland China is just 10% of that of Taiwan. The salaries of everyone from the factory security guards to the plant manager are 10% of those in Taiwan. As for those industries that have remained in Taiwan to the present, if they still rigidly concentrate on how to reduce capital costs, increase automation, improve efficiency, and the like, in the long run they are focusing on not very crucial matters.

The correct way to solve their fundamental problems is for these enterprises to transform, change direction, transform into capital-intensive, technology-intensive and speed-intensive industries, or else settle on becoming related industries, satellite factories, or investors. Here are just a few workable means to achieve success.

Enlarge Capital Base

The next step is to enlarge the capital base. Greater capital is needed in an Industrial Society than in an Agricultural one. In a Network Society, even though enterprises now create wealth from knowledge, they still require more capital than they did in an Industrial Society. Nowadays, a semiconductor assembly line requires an initial investment of NT$25 billion, which would be the equivalent of the investment required to establish a steel plant. Therefore, in the Network Society, enlargement of the capital base is an absolute necessity.

Recruit Highly-Skilled Personnel

If enterprises want to reach the goals of technology-intensity and creativity-intensity, they need the efforts and cooperation of all kinds of highly-skilled personnel. Consequently, recruiting skilled personnel is an essential element in changing an enterprise's nature. Moreover, this is not just a matter of attracting talent from other companies by offering lucrative contracts. What's more important is how to give talented personnel enough authority so that they have space to develop and bring their ability and creativity into play: in this way, the enterprise can truly harness and benefit from their talent and potential.

Asia as our Hinterland

In recent years, Taiwan enterprises have talked about internationalization. As a matter of fact, many factories in Taiwan have no way to take the plunge to realizing genuine internationalization. Internationalization starts within the neighborhood; local enterprises must first take Asia as their hinterland.

During our first economic miracle, we took Taiwan itself as our hinterland in selling products on the international market. Now that we have greater capacity, we need to take Asia as our hinterland in order to effectively harness all the resources, component parts and manpower available there. In this way, we can rapidly upgrade our scale of operations, our business prospects, and our creativity.

The China Market

In 1976, at the close of the Cultural Revolution in China, Deng Xiaoping appeared on the scene to orchestrate the reform movement. By the late 1980s, China had formed a stable economic base.

After Taiwan authorities opened the door to investments in China in 1990, many Taiwanese businessmen went to China to make investments there because, by that time, there was no reason not to allow investments.

As a matter of fact, even before investments were allowed, some businessmen had already begun to make investments in China. Taiwanese businessmen act quickly! By the end of the 1980s, well before the government had opened the door to investments in China, many Taiwanese businessmen had gone to China and discovered it to be an ideal place to make investments. As more and more information became available from people who had gone there, more and more people went to China to invest.

Still, everyone should understand one point: in the past, many Taiwanese businessmen had either worked their way up from rags to riches, or from blue-collar workers to prosperous business owners. If these companies had attempted to invest in a place like, say, an island in the Caribbean Sea, and had to manage foreign employees there, they would have run into severe difficulties. We simply lacked the English ability and management systems to manage foreign employees.

As to investing in China, however, we found no big differences in language and culture. Many Taiwanese businessmen who invested in China found they could use the old management methods they had used in Taiwan.

Consequently, Mainland China became the best place for Taiwanese businessmen to invest. For this reason, within a five-year period a large portion of Taiwan manufacturers moved their operations to Mainland China. By recent estimates, over 30,000 Taiwanese businessmen have gone to China to invest.

Indeed, China is a convenient place for us to make

investments. Despite the many critical discussions and analyses of the risks of investing there, China has been a sort of black hole, continuously sucking in Taiwanese businessmen during the past several years.

This is why the problem of how to apply our China investment policy effectively is another essential precondition for successfully developing a second economic miracle in Taiwan.

Youth Enterprise

At present, there is a special phenomenon in Taiwan. That is, while it is middle and old aged people who start up businesses, their market often is young people.

Thus, for many businesses, such as KTVs and bowling alleys, youth make up the principal customers. This phenomenon is just the opposite of the first economic miracle. We need to quickly change things around.

People who have already made their fortune should start to play the role of investor or consumer and offer more encouragement to youth to start up businesses of their own. They shouldn't think that youth don't have what it takes to succeed. Recall that twenty or thirty years ago we, too, were young. At the time, our elders thought we couldn't make a go of it, but we still created Taiwan's first economic miracle.

I have a friend who still goes to work everyday, even though he is 50 or 60 years old. I told him, "You don't need to work. You have plenty of money; you might as well let young people work." He replied, "I can't. My son is still a university student."

I thought to myself that his thinking was not entirely accurate. This is no longer the Agricultural Age. We no longer have to bequeath all our work or trade to our children. We can bequeath things like wealth, real estate, and stock to our children, but enterprises are public instruments, so it is best to leave them to the deserving, to the capable.

How to select new leaders from among the talented youth in our enterprise to carry the torch, how to give them authority, and how to make them the heirs of our enterprise - are all very important matters. We all need to have these kinds of concepts and magnanimity if we are to take our economic miracle to an even higher level.

Government Assistance

Finally, assistance from our government is a necessary condition for the success of a second economic miracle. Government assistance simply cannot be left out of the equation.

Taiwanese manufacturers don't have the ability to create an economic miracle by themselves. Just as the first economic miracle resulted from the cooperative efforts of the government and the people, it will again take the common purpose and joint efforts of Taiwanese enterprises and the government to create a second economic miracle.

Our expectations for government assistance are as follows:--

(Taiwan's Silicon Valley: Taipei to Hsin-chu)

First, the government should promote the establishment of Taiwan's Silicon Valley. At present, while there are quite a lot of hi-tech companies located between Hsin-chu and Taipei, there has been no systematic planning. There is no mass rapid transit system or high- speed network linking Hsin-chu and

Taipei. For hi-tech industries, this is a major drawback. The government really should make big plans to develop the infrastructure there, so that those industries can sustain steady growth.

In the past, we advocated developing Taiwan into a hi-tech island. I, too, recommended this idea. But, a hi-tech island is just a concept. To realize this idea, to establish the industrial capability, requires the concentration of optimal conditions. Even a vast country like the United States has to concentrate its hi-tech industry in a single region: Silicon Valley. This concentration of hi-tech manufacturers facilitates the flow, transfer and provision of all sorts of resources.

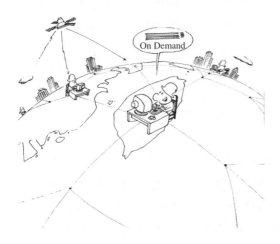

Consequently, we should understand that the expression "hi-tech island" serves to indicate the optimal direction of Taiwan's overall economic development. And, with regards to industrial planing, companies should concentrate their facilities and operations to avoid wasting resources and time on transportation.

(High Speed Network: on receipt -> on demand)

Fundamentally, the high-speed network marks a watershed between the Network Society and the Industrial Society. When we spoke of a watershed in the past, the watershed between the Agricultural Society and the Industrial Society was the introduction of a highway network and railroad lines.

While the word 'network' is no longer considered a new word, or new technology, it is mankind's new method for absorbing information.

At present, all of our methods for absorbing information take the form of "on receipt." A newspaper delivered to our door when we get up in the morning, programs broadcast when we turn on the television, and what we see walking down the street: in every case, all we see is what other people want us to see. A consumer may not be able to see what he wants to see. While on a network, he can gather a lot of information from various servers. That is, simply by connecting his computer to the telephone lines, a consumer can actively select the information he wants to see. This is called an "on demand" system.

This is not simply a new technology or a new fashion. It marks the transition from the traditional "on receipt" to the new "on demand," when you can obtain exactly what you want and what you need. The difference between them lies in the fact that active reception of information is the systematic accumulation of knowledge, instead of passive reception of information. This will benefit the information integration of society as a whole.

(Integrate PC and IC Industries)

The PC industry and the IC industry are two of Taiwan's most "futuristic" industries. They are already well established. By adding more integration, it would be easy to create more wealth and work opportunities.

As a matter of fact, Taiwan's investment in

manpower and money in the PC and IC industries, as well as the profits earned by these two industries, have already greatly influenced the people's livelihood here. Yet, investment in the PC industry has focused on importing key components and technology for mid- and down- stream assembly and re-export on behalf of major international OEMs. The IC industry is also established on a base emphasizing foundry (OEM) service. We are definitely doing well in these endeavors. However, when we compare our earnings with the profits gained by large international companies, we can describe our share using the old saying, "While others eat meat, we drink soup."

If Taiwan expects to become a worldwide key player in the computer industry, the integration of its PC and IC industries will be a decisive factor. With the integration of these two industries, Taiwan could have "complete production lines" for computers and achieve a more independent status. In this way, Taiwan's influence on the international computer market and ability to use the PC and IC industries to create wealth would be greatly enhanced.

(Develop Supercomputers)

Now that the computer industry is the main driving force in the creation of a second economic miracle, in the eyes of computer manufacturers, the government must be more advanced and more acute.

At present, Taiwan's computer companies already possess first-rate, world-class computer manufacturing and design technology. But, government participation has been inadequate. The government should offer the vision and planning to stimulate Taiwan's computer industry and lead it to a higher level. Promoting the development of a supercomputer would be an effective way to reach that objective.

At present, Taiwan's research institutes are conducting their computer research efforts pretty much along the same lines as private industries, which is nothing very significant. But, for the government to sponsor development of a supercomputer would be significant in two respects: it would (1) establish our national image, and (2) stimulate the overall development of our hi-tech technology.

Establishing the national image is something that the government should undertake. Taiwan already has advanced computer production technology, but we can't shake our national image as a country of OEMs

(Original Equipment Manufacturing). Developing supercomputers would put Taiwan's computer technology at the center of world attention. No matter the costs, the government should pool all resources and gather all experts and at full speed, start developing the fastest and the most advanced supercomputer.

In fact, developing a supercomputer would require a budget of a mere several hundred million US dollars. At present, the planned budget dispersed among various research units in Taiwan is about this amount. Thus, the project of developing a supercomputer need not add to the government's financial burden.

In the computer industry, giant companies like IBM or Intel can independently develop a super computer. Indeed, they have gained a lot of attention around the world because they have successfully created supercomputers. Furthermore, Taiwan's government has a capability greater than that of these computer companies, which makes developing a supercomputer within our ability.

If Taiwan were to start developing a supercomputer, this would be a significant development of Taiwan's future for both Taiwan and the entire computer world.

Of course, it is uncertain whether we will be able to chart our own course in the future. Be that as it may, we still shouldn't be guilty of "lack of initiative."

(Retraining Engineering)

Retraining is an important means of upgrading the capabilities of enterprises and individuals. Many enterprises are working hard on promoting on-the-job training for employees. However, that is not enough. We need the government to sponsor retraining work concerning social transformation.

Mr. John C. I. Ni, Director General of the Small and Medium Enterprise Administration of Ministry of Economic Affairs, has been doing some of this work, but the scope needs to expanded.

At present, many of our enterprises have moved their operations to Mainland China. Their employees who originally worked at making shoes and umbrellas are ill prepared to start working in semiconductor or computer companies. Their problem is that they have lost their jobs, and society's problem is that this productive force is standing idle and wasted. Therefore, society's retraining of industrial workers should be the government's response to economic transformation. Thus, as we are transforming from an industrial economy into a network economy, retraining is an important issue to consider. Our government must plan ahead to keep in step with the times. It must plan and promote a well-rounded retraining program, lest we should make the same mistake as Japan - not realizing that this is a big problem until it is too late.

(Introduce International Topics and Knowledge)

In the past, the government played the role of attracting capital. Now in the age of using knowledge to create wealth, the government should play the new role of attracting knowledge. What's even more important is keeping abreast of leading international topics and absorbing timely international knowledge.

We now have the feeling that we are living in a global village. When everyone overseas is discussing international environmental protection (ISO 14000) and intellectual property rights, Taiwan cannot afford to swim against the current. Taiwan has to swim with these currents; otherwise, we will be unable to conduct international business. We cannot take the attitude that

these currents don't match
the situation in our country
and therefore stay isolated
from international society.
That is the wrong attitude.
Government and enterprises
alike have to prepare an open
international personality and
outlook.

*(Institute for Intellectual
Property Rights)*

The present age takes
intellectual property rights
very seriously. Even when we
are using knowledge to
create wealth nowadays, we
cannot neglect to respect
intellectual property rights.
Because of this, I advocate
that the government set up
an expert unit exclusively
responsible for handling

1 5 3

intellectual property rights issues. My idea is to set up an "Institute for Intellectual Property Rights." Why do I propose an "Institute" for intellectual property rights? I think this matter is important enough to warrant an institute that would command the same respect as, say, the "Institute for Information Industry."

Intellectual property rights will become more and more important for future industries intensive in capital, technology and speed. If we don't resolve the intellectual property rights issue soon, we will become more and more deeply caught up in it. The day of reckoning will come sooner or later. When our companies have grown large and profitable, foreign companies holding essential intellectual property rights will come and request us to pay for the use of their intellectual property. The bigger our enterprise, the more they will ask. Once we infringe upon their intellectual property rights, we will incur grievous losses.

Therefore, we must look at an institute for intellectual property rights as seriously as we have looked upon the Institute for Information Industry; we should treat them with equal importance. We should focus on how to prevent our businesses from infringing on the intellectual property rights of others, how to settle such disputes legally once they break out, how to protect people's creative ideas, how to promote the recognition of intellectual property rights, etc. All of these responsibilities should be taken up by an institute for intellectual property rights, a possible government organization of the future.

(Technology Diplomacy)

A country like Taiwan should not think that money can buy friends, or that a country with money doesn't need to have friends. Foreign relations are still very important.

We want to sell our products everywhere overseas. Even if our government lacks international recognition or status, we still want to coexist with others in the world, so we definitely need to strengthen our foreign relations.

Our government's foreign relations suffer great interference from China and we encounter snags and difficulties everywhere, that is why some people advocate "economic diplomacy." In fact, economic relations are also difficult to maintain. This has been especially apparent recently when people have been feeling distressed and disgusted with bribery and the misuse of money. Relying on wealth alone to establish foreign relations is certainly not the way to solve our problems.

I prefer to think that we can work toward expanding our technological diplomacy. During the past thirty years we have accumulated many kinds of technology. In many areas we have become world a leader. If we can transplant technologies to countries like Thailand and Malaysia, we can also transplant technologies to other countries around the world.

The difference between money and technology is that technology can be duplicated. Moreover, the original technology and the duplicated technology can be used at the same time. If we give NT$50 million to another country, we no longer possess that $50 million. While, if we hand umbrella-making technology over to, say, Thailand, we would not be prevented from producing umbrellas in Venezuela or Panama. In this way, using technology to make true friends is a practical program that we can try from now on. At the same time, our manufacturers can increase their income while they take their technology to other places. Thus, this would be a win-win policy.

(Cross-Straits Peace)

No matter what political system and concepts we finally adopt, no matter who finally governs, we definitely need to maintain cross-straits peace. A Taiwan overshadowed by the thunder of cannon fire would have no way to create another economic miracle.

During the past thirty or forty years, Chinese people in Taiwan, working with extremely primitive equipment and methods, managed to create, step by step, Taiwan's first economic miracle. Today we operate under such favorable conditions, such as ample financial resources, a vast reserve of technological talent, open channels of information, creative entrepreneurs that we need not waste energy criticizing or struggling over some minor negative problems; we should put all our energy into advancing towards the future.

(Optimistically Welcome the Future)

I am not overly optimistic. I also don't believe that the next economic miracle can occur without our making a concerted effort. However, I can see the rise of a new turning point in Taiwan's industries. As in the painstaking effort of creating the first economic miracle of the past, with the cooperative efforts of enterprises and government, I believe that we have a chance to create "Taiwan's Second Economic Miracle," a miracle that will benefit all Chinese people.

Before he passed away in 1975, the eminent British historian, Professor Arnold Toynbee, predicted that the 21st century would be a Chinese century. Let's strive together to make Professor Toynbee's prediction become a reality.

If it is said that, in human history, the 21st century will be the Asian century; well, that would not be so startling.

Professor Arnold Toynbee
1899-1975

The Seventh Movement: Taiwan's Strongest Industry in 2001

Which industry will be the strongest in Taiwan in 2001? What will be the bottleneck in the growth of Taiwan's enterprises? Since we always mention creativity, what will be the connection between creativity and Taiwan's strongest industry in 2001?

Taiwan's Strongest Industry in 2001

There are two criteria we can adopt in weighing the strength of industries in Taiwan. The first is foreign sales. An enterprise's sales in the domestic market are usually influenced by scale of investment, timeliness of investment, relationship with the government and other factors. However, foreign market sales require real competitiveness in the international arena. As a result, we can say foreign sales volume is an important evaluation criterion. The other criterion is performance, or return on capital.

During the 1990s, Taiwan's strongest industries were its capital-intensive, technology-intensive and speed-intensive computers and semiconductor industries. In 1997, eight of Taiwan's top ten exporting businesses were capital-, technology- and speed-intensive manufacturers. The top ten enterprises in performance were all involved in information electronics.

In the early 1990s, those who were able to foresee capital-intensive, technology-intensive and speed-intensive industries became Taiwan's strongest industries later on in the decade. Investors in them have obviously been able to reap immense profits.

Today, at the beginning of the year 2000, which industry will be Taiwan's strongest in 2001? Before answering, let us discuss the direction of Taiwan's strongest capital-, technology- and speed-intensive industries.

I. Development Bottleneck of Taiwan Capital-, Technology-, and Speed-intensive Industries

Presently, Taiwan's strongest capital-, technology- and speed-intensive industries are the computer and semiconductor industries. The computer and semiconductor industries have produced many rapidly rising large-scale companies. These companies have been predicted to enjoy continued growth during the coming two to three years. But, when business revenues start to approach NT$100 billion, these companies might begin to encounter growth bottlenecks.

The main reason for this is that, except for Acer, most of Taiwan's computer companies are mainly Original Design Manufacturers (ODM). If these companies want to sustain continued strong growth, they need large scale manufacturing contracts.

However, there is a definite limit to the number of contracts that can be made in the computer world. In addition to large scale manufacturing contracts, these companies need to enjoy an ever closer relationship with their customers, so that they may grow together. Because of this situation, a company might find itself in the difficult situation of dealing with many competing customers at the same time. Therefore, we can see a developing pattern of joint ventures between Taiwan's large-scale computer companies and large-scale international computer companies. Our business growth will come to depend more upon on a customer's scale of business and cooperative relationship, which can potentially form bottlenecks in business sales growth. Unless the scale of major computer companies continues to grow steadily, most of the Taiwan's large-scale computer suppliers will quite possibly encounter a growth bottleneck when business revenues reach about NT$100 billion.

Semiconductor companies have made the largest investments and the greatest profits over the past ten years. At present, the principal business of most semiconductor companies here is the production of memories and wafers. In the wake of East Asia's financial storm, South Korea's currency depreciated greatly. Korea already had a hold on the world memory market, but after their currency devaluation, they were able to reduce prices and have now become even more competitive. Because of this, Taiwan's semiconductor companies will turn to the more profitable business of making wafers. Consequently, with too many companies competing for this business, both the profitability of wafer manufacturers as a whole and the sales growth of each individual company will be affected. Companies that are currently doing high volume business may not want to engage in excessive price-slashing competition. As a result, they will face a bottleneck in their business growth.

Because of this situation, we can see that around the year 2000, Taiwan's most successful capital-, technology- and speed-intensive industries of the 1990s will face serious bottlenecks in their growth.

What growth strategy should these companies adopt for the first decade of the 21st century? Recently, Mr. Stan Shih, the leader of Taiwan's computer industry, and Mr. Morris Chang, the leader of Taiwan's semiconductor industry both expressed the same idea -creativity - at the Century Seminar.

II. Creativity-intensity

The secret for Taiwan's three-intensive industries to continue to enjoy steady growth into the first decade is for them to be "creativity-intensive." What, then, is "creativity?" And, what is "creativity-intensity?"

1. The Value of Creativity in Industries

The significance of the term "creativity" includes creating new ideas, creating new products, creating new technologies, and much more. Its scope is quite broad.

In an industry, there are three necessary conditions for a creative idea to be transformed into business value:

a. Technical Feasibility

I have a good friend from America. He is the vice president of a well-known international information statistics company. One day he called to tell me that he had an idea for a new product.

When we got together he became very excited and told me that if this idea could be made into a product, we could sell millions, or perhaps even tens of millions of units. Before telling me his idea, he hoped I would first promise that if we decided to make such a product I would give him a definite royalty.

I replied that I couldn't make such a promise because it would have no legal basis. I could just promise that if his idea was feasible, and if nobody else had come up with this idea, we could begin to discuss the details of cooperation.

He smiled and said, "Alright. I believe you." Thereupon, he began to explain his idea: it would be a handheld device, the front would be a liquid crystal display (LCD) screen, and the back would be a little document scanner. You would just need to put a name card under the scanner to scan the details into the device. Afterwards, one could

Creativity-intensity

Creative thoughts and concepts are the essential factors to spur Taiwan's second economic miracle.

display the name card information on the screen on demand. Thus, the device would function as an electronic name cardholder and save us the trouble of carrying a lot of name cards around. A little computer inside the device would arrange the name card data, and retrieve requested name card data on demand.

After listening patiently to his description of the product, I playfully said, "Your idea is a pretty good one. If we were to propose it in to a company, we could win a prize of about sixty US dollars."

I then proceeded to open the file of employee new product ideas in my notebook computer to show him some similar prize winning ideas. I explained to him that, although someday we might have the technology to make these product ideas feasible, we didn't have suitable technology to produce them yet. For example, scanners nowadays use a lot of electricity. It would exhaust the unit's batteries just to scan in about five name cards! Moreover, how could we render the name card data in a standard uniform form, so that they could be retrieved from the unit's data bank? That would be another difficult problem to tackle.

In the industry's view, no matter how outstanding or visionary an idea might be, if it is not technically feasible, it is just as useless as Rose's brilliant diamond necklace, the "Star of the Sea," in *Titanic*, lying alone at the bottom of the sea.

b. Market Acceptance

For a "creative idea" to produce value in an industry, besides being technically feasible, most importantly, it must win market acceptance.

A dog food manufacturer once developed a fragrant new dog food product. But, after a marketing campaign, sales did not measure up to expectations. Consequently, the company president called a meeting of all top level management and the marketing and sales department to discuss the problem. He hoped to discover the reason why the product performed poorly on the market, so that he could find a way to strengthen sales.

In the meeting, a section manager reported that due to the high retail price the product was not competitive on the market. Next, a senior manager reported that not enough was spent on advertising, so the product had too little market recognition. A vice president then advocated getting some dog movie stars to model for television commercials, and so the discussion went.

Although the people at the meeting came up with many proposals, the company president still did not feel satisfied. Just when he was beginning to lose patience, he noticed a sales employee sitting in the back, with his head hanging down, looking rather despondent. The company president suddenly called out his name and said, "Tell us what you think. Why isn't this new dog food performing well on the market?" The young employee looked as if he'd been suddenly stirred from his sleep. He then stammered, somewhat nervously, "Isn't it because... dogs... dogs...won't eat it?"

A dog food that dogs won't eat certainly won't do well on the market.

This example vividly reminds us that, even if a good creative idea is technically feasible, it will be useless if it doesn't enjoy a good reception on the market.

This sort of situation often occurs with ideas proposed by engineers.

Most engineers around the world come up with ideas in light of technical feasibility, but they tend to overlook market acceptance.

Dr. Casper Shih, who has made significant contributions to upgrading the productivity of enterprises in Taiwan, once told a very moving story. He said there was a drunkard searching for his keys under a street light. He searched half the night but still couldn't find them. A policeman who saw him walked over and asked, "What are you looking for?" The drunkard answered, "I'm looking for the keys I dropped." "Where did you drop them?" "I dropped them near my front door." The policeman felt this was odd, and then asked, "If you dropped them near your front door, why are you looking for them here?" The drunkard answered, "I am looking for them here because there is no light near my front door. There is light here, so I will be able to see them."

Very often, we conduct our research and development in obvious and convenient places, but neglect places where we really can come up with something. That is why we tend to form creative ideas that are technically feasible, but fail to consider market acceptance.

c. Legal Protection

The fact that a creative idea is both technically feasible and can enjoy broad market acceptance doesn't guarantee that it will be a money-making idea. This is especially true when we neglect to secure legal protection on what is called "intellectual property rights," because creative ideas can be plagiarized and pirated on a large scale. There is often no way for the original manufacturer to reclaim its lost earnings and recoup its investment.

Problems of this kind occur when we have not secured legal protection. Examples of grievous losses due to a lack of legal protection have been especially common in the electronic information industry.

In 1981, when IBM decided to use Microsoft's operating system software, MS DOS, IBM neglected

Thinking...
Thinking...

New Idea

to secure the co-copyright of the software. As a result, the cooperation turned out to be IBM endorsing Microsoft's software with IBM's 100-year reputation, which helped Microsoft's operating system become the international standard for personal computers. While Microsoft was enjoying its great success, IBM not only had to continue paying Microsoft huge royalties, but IBM's standing in the computer industry became threatened by Microsoft.

One minor legal oversight can lead to "one misstep, endless regrets."

2. The Source of Creative Ideas

"Creativity" refers mainly to new creative ideas, technologies and products. Creative ideas can come from momentary inspiration. But, creativity does not only result from free play of the imagination. For an enterprise, the sources of creativity can be methodically managed.

a. Information Gathering

Patent Gazette gathers the world's latest, most feasible ideas. A reader familiar with the contents of this publication will know what creative ideas have been proposed, what new ideas are under serious consideration, and what ideas might become industry trendsetters. Besides this, the contents of *Patent Gazette* let us know what other people have done, so that we needn't proceed to develop the same creative idea. In this way, we can save a lot of time and avoid some false leads.

Gathering sufficient information like this is a basic requirement for coming up with creative ideas. Because of this, we need to have a team of experts read *Patent Gazette* to analyze and synthesize this information to find any creative ideas that might be beneficial to or even vital to the company.

The Japanese always devote themselves to gathering information. What's most important, however, is that they know how to digest this information.

One year I went to the United States to participate in a major consumer electronics show (CES Show), which was an extremely important exhibition in the international consumer electronics business. In addition, it was a prime venue for publicizing the latest products and gathering the latest technology for the industry.

That year, Toshiba dispatched a forty-member delegation to participate in the exhibition. These forty people were divided into a technology team and a business team. Each time, one team would go into the exhibition to get information. When the team had gathered enough information, it would return and then the other team would study and find out why certain new products were considered important or creative. At this point, they would ask the first team some questions. These questions and answer sessions were constructed so that the engineers could get the views of the business market. At the same time, those involved in sales could learn some basic technology concepts. "Creativity" can be likened to inhaling or digesting. This method of having production line people and sales take in the latest product and technology information was extremely effective. Reflecting back, many Taiwanese companies typically just sent their boss to these exhibitions. They would then rush around the exhibition gathering information. Afterwards, they would report back in vague and impressionistic terms on what they gathered, to their employees. This approach, of course, makes it difficult to select the best of the creative ideas, not to mention developing them into viable new products. Thus, the reason why Taiwanese enterprises have not been very successful at continuously developing new products is that our information gathering efforts have not been adequate.

b. Brainstorming

Gathering information allows us to have sufficient knowledge. Brainstorming, then, is a way to set off everybody's sparks of creativity. By this method, we can quickly concentrate on several assorted ideas that show ways to make a creative idea feasible.

I have heard that Sony Corporation always holds a "brainstorming banquet" after work on Fridays. Anyone who attends may express any idea he or she wants to. People never say "no" at these gatherings. Anyone can make a statement as he or she pleases, and everyone is free to converse. These brainstorming banquets are entirely recorded on video. Then, on the following Monday, the tapes are viewed to see whether or not any feasible ideas had come up.

c. Matrix Scanning (Encircling the Sea to Net Fish)

"Creative ideas" are not necessarily "new inventions." Some existing creative ideas can be used in various products to create surprising results. To modify an application is also a form of creative thinking. To systematically consider alternative applications is called matrix scanning.

In the past, television screens were not so big. The most popular size television screen that enjoyed the greatest sales was 20 inches. Afterwards, with advances in technology, larger televisions with 26- inch screens that were easier on the eyes began to outsell the 20-inch models. Before long, 29-inch televisions began to outsell the 26-inch models. Because people began to keep at least two television sets at home, the entire television market was able to expand with the introduction of these large screen sets. Naturally, it was easier than usual for the person who came up with this creative idea to be a success.

"Enlarging the screen" indeed was not a bad idea. And, this creative idea was applied to computer monitors, calculators, electronic dictionaries, PDAs, and similar electronic products. This approach is somewhat like fishing. Suppose you land a fish in a certain fishing spot. If you then set up nets around this spot to net even more fish, that is what is called encircling the sea to net fish.

The strength of this approach is that it allows you to save a lot of time searching around for "feasible" ideas. Someone in Taiwan looked at an ice cream cake and thought, "since we can make ice cream cakes, we should be able to make moon cakes stuffed with ice cream." After ice cream moon cakes sold well on the market, many other ice cream products that previously didn't have ice cream inside began to appear in the market. Food companies certainly have made money from this idea and, at the same time, benefited customers, who now have more delicious selections to enjoy.

3. Creative Employees

An established enterprise always has R&D and planning units, manned with experts responsible for creative work. That is not always enough, though. In capital-, technology-, speed- and creativity-intensive industries of the future, farsighted entrepreneurs will treat every employee as a source of creative ideas and provide him or her with opportunities to develop creative ideas.

One event made a deep impression on me.

One night two years ago, I went to a nightclub with several people, who were in the same field of business as I was. We wanted to sing karaoke and unwind after a hard day's work. After we were seated, a waiter brought us tea and towels. Meanwhile, a "princess" spoke in a familiar way to one of us, " Chairman Chang! Long time no see. Do you still remember me?" Mr. Chang was a little embarrassed and a little surprised, because he really did recognize the "princess." She was Miss Lee, a fine-featured girl, who had once worked as an assembly line worker in his company.

Even though Chang hadn't done much drinking that night, he gradually seemed to get a little tipsy.

Whenever Miss Lee came over to serve us, Chang would look as though he wanted to say something after she left our table.

Afterwards, he couldn't restrain himself any longer. Somewhat stirred up, he patted my shoulder and said,

"Chairman Wen, our society really has come to this. Even good girls like her give up regular jobs and come to places like this to work. Isn't that so? Isn't it?" I understood clearly how Chang felt. At the time, I just smiled and didn't reply, but in my heart I didn't think he was right.

Chairman Chang's company is a hi-tech company that earns several billion NT dollars per year. If a high earning company like this not only cannot keep its employees, but also let its employees run off to work in a karaoke bar or a nightclub, it suggests that that company has not fulfilled its obligation to society. You would have to reflect on whether the problem wasn't perhaps that you hadn't let your employees have a decent share in the company's ample earnings. Don't just blame social customs and personal morality.

Someone might say she was just an assembly line worker, so how could she expect to receive a high salary?

Before I answer this question, let me tell a famous story.

Henry Ford, the great American auto magnate once

took a picture, which later became very famous. In that picture, Henry Ford was elated and behind him was an assembly line of several hundred workers. The caption at the bottom read: "some of them only need to use a hand or a foot to do their job."

In the Industrial Age, strict division of labor was an essential feature of mass production.

Ford must have been quite proud when he said that, because he had used this assembly line approach to break through eons of history to achieve real mass production on an impressive scale. In this way, with the help of machines, humanity could reach levels of productivity that would have been unimaginable in the Agricultural Age. In the Network Age, however, this simple use of employees' hands and eyes and strict division of labor are no longer a trend.

If we realize that a person's potential is unlimited, then even if a worker seems to be doing fine in his or her present job, he or she still might have many other talents that the enterprise should help to develop. Take a pretty young assembly line worker with a bright personality as an example. There are many things she could do, such as working at product exhibitions or publicity events, or even using her special feel for beauty in all the areas the company could make best use of.

My mentor, Dr. Sasaki, the father of Japan's electronic calculators, discovered in his recent research that women tend to have possibly over 30% more brain cells than men do. This explains why women are highly perceptual and have a fairly reliable intuition in real life situations that men cannot comprehend. He concluded that if women could bring their superior sense of perception into play at work, the creativity and effect would be unimaginable for that enterprise. Our best example of this is Tamagotchi.

Tamagotchi was invented by a Japanese female. Strictly speaking, Tamagotchi was not just a matter of transferring our love for animals into an electronic product. Even though the creative idea and technology of this product was quite simple, hundreds of millions of Tamagotchis had been sold worldwide, causing a serious shortage of IC units in the world market. Tamagotchi has become a social phenomenon. Reflecting a subtle change in psychology and attitude in the electronics world, a simple product with this sort of effect could not have been created through ordinary common sense.

4. Creative Culture

In order to encourage creativity in the capital-, technology-, speed- and creativity-intensive hi-tech industries, enterprises absolutely must forge a sort of unique and enthusiastic creative culture.

Enterprises cannot afford to just pay lip service to the idea of creative culture. They must hold their own creativity conferences, and encourage all their employees to attend and be more creative.

At a company meeting, I listened to Inventec's Group President Richard Lee explain in detail the company's method for encouraging creativity to his employees. Besides its Research and Development Department and Planning Department, manned with experts responsible for conceiving and planning new products, Inventec has also established a complete creativity reward system. They have also set up a series of classes to teach employees how to write up their creative idea proposals. From time to time, these creative idea proposals are publicized by posting on the network, and a prize is offered for good ideas (whether they are implemented or not). Three level creativity prizes awarded to employees include an idea adoption prize and an intellectual property rights prize. If an employee were to score top points for each creativity encouragement prize item, he or she could earn up to an extra NT$430,000 per month. I believe that with this method of providing concrete rewards and a real sense of accomplishment, every employee will feel motivated to research and develop ideas on his own, without thinking that he or she is depending just on his or her original hard-earned salary to make this "easier" money. From the company's point of view, it is fulfilling a social responsibility.

III. Taiwan's Capital-, Technology-, Speed-, and Creativity-intensive Industries (Four-intensive Industries)

Standing at the onset of the Third Wave-the Network Society-we have enough reasons to believe that by around the year 2000 the development of Taiwan's hi-tech industries will advance in the overall trend toward capital-, technology-, speed-, and creativity-intensive industries.

Because Taiwan's electronics industry operates mainly under the ODM (Original Design Manufacturing) model, the trend will be toward having more one-to-one cooperative relationships for production with established cooperative manufacturers. We might be able to see some more new enterprises emerging, but given the limited scale of the global electronics market, even if Taiwan's electronic information manufacturers can expect a good future, I fear that individual companies will face the NT$ 100 billion barrier.

The reason for this is very simple. There are few electronics firms in the world whose revenues reach NT$100 billion. Furthermore, a world-class manufacturer is unlikely to rely on one single vendor for all products' designing and manufacturing.

In order to break through this bottleneck, Taiwan's electronics enterprises will have to change their passive stance to an active stance in order to rapidly develop a competitive advantage of creativity intensiveness. In other words, they must change their corporate production style from that of ODM (Original Design Manufacturing) to that of OIM (Original Idea Manufacturing).

Taiwan presently depends on its unique capital-, technology-, and speed-intensity abilities to be a mass volume ODM unit, well beyond the reach of Japan,

South Korea, and Hong Kong. This also has allowed Taiwan's electronics industry to flourish. On the other hand, manufacturers who have engaged in cooperative ODM production have taken a passive stance. Moreover, this can easily result in competition between local enterprises in the same industry. With everyone competing on an equal footing with three-intensive conditions, the ones offering the lowest prices will be the ones most likely to win opportunities to cooperate with large foreign companies, which will be the sole winners benefiting from the situation.

OIM, on the other hand, can change our passive stance into an active stance. When we evaluate an enterprise's performance in the future, we won't simply look at revenues. What will be more important will be how many patents, copyrights and intellectual property rights that a company holds.

The more intellectual property rights an enterprise holds, even if it produces nothing itself, the larger the profits from manufacturers that use intellectual property rights.

An enterprise with the ability to obtain intellectual property rights and create creativity-intensiveness will be able to develop its own unique, strong products.

Once a company's products have the additional advantages of speed and advanced technology, the big companies with whom a company had originally cooperated in the past would turn around to purchase its products. This would result in a deeper cooperative relationship between a particular company and its buyer. Having made products for a buyer, a company understands the buyer better. But, if a particular company's powerful products were to be purchased by a buyer's rivals, that would pose a survival risk for the original buyer. In the meanwhile, if a particular company displayed strong ability and competitiveness on the market, other companies would flock to cooperate with it.

Because of this, if one were to claim that the NT$100 billion scale is the definite "rooftop" of present day capital-, technology-, and speed-intensive industries in Taiwan, I would say that "creativity-intensity" would be the most effective way of removing that roof. And, once that rooftop was removed, the scale we could attain would be incalculable, because an enterprise with its own creativity would be able to enjoy unlimited development.

Intel provides the best example of this. This

hardware company which produces some 80% of the CPUs in the world enjoys annual profits that reach US$6

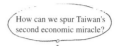

billion. The company's secret weapon of success is not just that it continuously increases the speed of CPU calculations, but that it continuously develops new software ideas for inside a CPU.

Given the rapid evolutionary trend of continuously upgrading electronic functions matched by continuous reductions in price, we must grasp the creativity-intensity ability as early as possible in order to catch the OIM (Original Idea Manufacturing) tide. This is how Taiwan's present capital-, technology-, and speed-intensive industries can maintain their competitive advantage and, when greeting the new century, be the true victors in the coming Third Wave - Network Age.

Appendix

The following speech Mr. Wen gave to the top management of Toshiba and Inventec at Xian, Mainland China in December, 1993.

The Zero "Lead-Time" Age

Zero Lead-time -- material flows like tap water.

During my childhood in the countryside, it was a major task to carry water home. We kids had to draw water from a well, into a bucket, stumble with the bucket all the way to the kitchen and pour the water into a large tub. By the time we reached the kitchen, the bucket was only about 70% full, so we had to make many trips back and forth to bring back enough water for a single day's use. My greatest dream then was to have a faucet from which water would flow at the turn of a tap.

Now that I am working in the electronics industry, my greatest dream is to have a material-flow system just like a tap-water-system— one that is available anytime without requiring any in-house storage. I call this idea of mine "zero lead-time".

The Ideal State of Zero Lead-time

Material ┆→Parts Maker＞Set Maker ＞Set Distributor┆→**Market**
            (P)   **(S)**   **(D)**
＜Industry Material Flow＞

This chart can be referred to as the "PSD Material Flow Chart." Whenever we talk about industry production value of a product, this refers to the total sales amount of distributors of a product. For example, when we say the calculator industry has a global production value of US$2 billion, we mean the total value of calculators sold by all distributors in the world is US$2 billion. Distributors' sales amount includes the calculator makers' sales amount; and the calculator makers' sales amount in turn includes the parts makers' sales amount. These relationships are shown in the chart below:

When viewed from the other end of the PSD chart, material that has not entered the parts maker's production process is not calculated into the industry's production value. Thus: The best method of "Cost Down" (cost cutting) is "never feed in materials for a product that doesn't sell."

The dotted lines in the PSD flow chart indicate the "Industry Material Flow." This is like the water stored in the pipeline between the water bureau's tank and the user's faucet. If we can feed in the materials at the same rate at which the distributors sell their final product, we have reached the ideal "zero lead-time" state.

The Global Just-In-Time Integrated System

Many factories push a Just-In-Time (JIT) program in order to streamline material flow and cut back on inventory. This practice is confined, however, to its own premises. Because manufacturers are not aware of a customers' inventory levels, when the market changes and the customer adjusts orders, the factories' own in-house Just-In-Time program will be severely disturbed and can only be achieved with limited success.

What we really need is a "Global Just-In-Time integrated System" shown in the PSD Chart, in order to achieve true zero lead-time. Let me reiterate: the most efficient "Cost Down" is not "zero inventory," but "never feed in materials for making products not yet ordered;

while delivering the necessary products immediately upon order."

The New Concept of "Lead-time"

Next, I would like to talk about several new concepts of "lead-time."

1. "The longer the lead-time, the greater the risk."

We used to think the longer the customer's purchase lead-time was, the more protective it would be for the supplier. A L/C on hand 90 days in advance meant safety. Today the reality is just the opposite.

Product life has changed from long to short, to very short, to unpredictable, because we have no way of telling what kind of new product competitors may unveil tomorrow. A new and improved product that is promoted through modern real-time media can drive current products out of the market overnight.

Let us say a customer gives you an L/C 90 days prior to delivery; there is a possibility that this product's life would end before you deliver it.

In such a case, from the PSD Chart, we could see that your product would not even enter the market; it would just flow downstream in the pipeline.

When a product's life ends unexpectedly, the following will occur:

*   The pipeline will be clogged. (Downstream customers will not be able to sell the product.)

*   The pipeline will become deformed (The best salesmen will have to try to sell a most un-sellable product.)

*   The market order will be destroyed. (The most un-sellable product will be forced into the market "at any cost.")

This may cause your company to stop factory production, or cause a delay in rolling out new products. The risk here is not lower than that of an order being canceled. This in turn leads us to another new concept.

2. "The longer the lead-time, the higher the cost."

Nowadays, the cost of winning the business of a new customer is far greater than that of changing a production line or rearranging production manpower. When a product life ends abruptly, we certainly try to go out to find new customers. This will inevitably increase our sales expenses, and possibly the number of salesmen. Consequently, on the one hand, we may reduce the number of operators on production lines. On the other hand, we will be forced to add several highly paid salesmen instead.

Under the prevailing profit-center management, we tend to overemphasize individual profit center's expenses while overlooking overall expenses. In an overcrowded and overcompetitive market, cutting down expenses is an essential source of profit.

Profit is generated here by
a. Reducing the number of customers (cut down our own expense), and
b. Increasing the order size (cut down customers' expense.)

3."The longer the lead-time, the higher the chance of poor judgment."

Today's industry has gradually evolved from being production-oriented to being new product-oriented. The success of the new product-oriented industry depends not on the company size, but on the speed with which it reacts to changes.

The long lead-time can diminish a company's alertness reaction time, reduce its ability to react to changes, and lead to poor judgments. The pace of change in today's market is tens times faster than it was twenty years ago. Ignoring the speed of change and sticking to the old habit of asking long lead-time is like an ostrich burying its head in the sand.

How to achieve zero lead-time?

Indeed, knowing what to do is our greatest challenge!

I propose dividing product lead-time into two basic stages: the Launch Stage and the Mass Production Stage.

1. Launch Stage

Let me emphasize here that the zero lead-time we are discussing applies to custom-made products only; for standardized products of a commodity-nature, asking lead-time is out of the question.

"Launch Stage" refers to the time it takes from product idea to the first batch of product introduced to the market. Consider our morning newspaper for example - at 8:00 PM the previous night editors stop taking in any more news; and the paper is delivered at 6:00 AM the next morning, to your doorstep. From this example we can realize how slow most other industries are. That is why I am pushing for concurrent engineering and relay development to cut down the time in the Launch Stage.

The Launch Stage requires a dedicated production line and a dedicated management system; everything here is designed for speed.

The Launch Stage is a key process in product planning. The Product Planning Group must take full responsibilities for its success. As for production capacity planning, if we forecast the launch quantity of 6,000 pcs, then:

2. Mass Production Stage

Zero lead-time does not mean "many models; small quantities." (Too many models are the result of poor product planning.) The proper concept is "a few models; appropriate quantities" - quantities in line with market demands.

How can we achieve zero lead-time during the mass production stage?

(1) "Real-time Information"

	1st (M)	2nd (M)	3rd (M)	4ht (M)
Traditional **(Production Oriented)**	**1,000**	**2,000**	**3,000**	**Actual** **Demand**
New **(Market Oriented)**	**6,000**	**0**	**0**	**Actual** **Demand**
	Launch Quantity			

The three parties in the PSD chart are connected by computer and communication systems. We can see the changes of numbers in real-time in the PSD chart. In other words, with these figures on hand, we will be able to control the material flows real-time, and this information will take the place of the physical inventory and its huge cost all together.

(2) "Dynamic Forecasting"

We should change from imprecise monthly forecasting like "50K this month, 60K next month, 100K the 3rd month..." to a more dynamic "weekly forecast," a "3-day forecast" or even a "daily forecast."

For a production line with a monthly capacity of 100K, there is no much difference between an order for "100K for the third month" and another order for "3~4K per day from the 60th day till the 90th day," except that the latter is more precise in terms of information management. Zero lead-time does not try to change the production time. Any production process takes a certain amount of time. Turning the faucet to make water flow does not mean that the water comes instantly from the bureau's storage tank.

In other words there is no need to continue to invest or substantially change current production. All we have to do is to change our mind-set and the method of information management. With the modern tools of computer and communication systems, we will be able to achieve zero lead-time!

The airline reservation system is a perfect example of "dynamic forecasting." Any passenger can cancel any reservation any time without any obligation. By using computer and communications technologies and precise information management, airlines can still cope with this unpredictability of the market and operate seamlessly.

Modern industries own huge amounts of capital investment and are equipped with many precision instruments, but many still regard the most important source of information - lead-time and production scheduling very heedlessly. We must once again turn our attention to this matter.

"Minimize the Loss of Redundant Inventory"

Even if we have done both the "Real-time Information" and "Dynamic Forecasting," we may still run out of luck: the product life is shorter than predicted, i.e. the product ends before all the material inventory in the PSD pipeline is used up. At this point, the most important thing to do is NOT to feed the redundant material into the production process, for this will only serve to further increase future cost; it is necessary to scrap the redundant materials on site so as to keep loss to a minimum.

After having done all of the above, theoretically, loss should be born by the Product Planning Group that is responsible for decision making (it could be any one of the PSD parties.)

What is the difference between people of the new generation and the old generation? If there is still some food left on the plate, the old generation will say, "Eat it all up, don't waste the food!" The new generation will say, "Leave the food, don't waste the body!"

Even though this may not be a perfect analogy, we should nevertheless dispose of redundant material with this new concept in mind.

NOW!

* The age in which the Parts maker, the Set maker, and the Distributor (PSD) limit each other's activities within a relationship of pure purchase and sale now belongs to the past.

* The age of zero lead-time is coming.

* The three parties that comprise PSD should cooperate more closely in order to maximize total profit in the industry they participate.

Always keep this in mind:

"My customer buys my product, not because of its low price or because of its good quality, or because of our good relationship; it is because he will be able to sell it for a good profit."

A *tomorrow* Book

Locus Publishing Company

Taipei County, Taiwan

11F, 25, Section 4, Nanking East Road, Taipei, Taiwan

ISBN 957-8468-50-4 Chinese Language Edition

ISBN 957-0316-61-6 English Language Edition

Copyright ©2001 by Sayling Wen &Tsai Chi-Chung

April 2001, First Edition

Printed in Taiwan

tomorrow11

Taiwan Prospect

作者：溫世仁　繪圖：蔡志忠

編輯：明日工作室

出版者：大塊文化出版股份有限公司

法律顧問：全理律師事務所董安丹律師

台北市105南京東路六段25號11樓

電話：(02)87123898 傳眞：(02)87123897

www.locuspublishing.com

e-mail:locus@locuspublishing.com

讀者服務專線：0800-006689

郵撥帳號：18955675 帳戶名：大塊文化出版股份有限公司

行政院新聞局局版北市業字第706號

總經銷：北城圖書有限公司　　地址：台北縣三重市大智路139號

電話：(02)29818089(代表號) 傳眞：(02)29883028 29813049

製版印刷：源耕印刷事業有限公司

初版一刷2001年4月　　定價：新台幣180元

版權所有‧翻印必究

Printed in Taiwan

LOCUS

LOCUS

LOCUS

LOCUS